One Plus One Equals Ten

One Plus One Equals Ten

A First Lady's Survival Guide for Stepmoms

Janice R. Love

Foreword by Dr. Bobby L. Love, Sr.

Divine
Garden
Press

Published by Divine Garden Press
P.O. Box 371
Soperton, GA 30457
www.divinegardenress.com

ISBN-13: 978-0615695389
ISBN-10: 0615695388
Library of Congress Control Number: 2012949054

Cover Design by A'ndrea J. Wilson
Cover Photo © Christiana Mustion

Contents

Introduction   **1**

One.   Dating With Children   **6**

Two.   One Big Happy Stepfamily   **23**

Three.   Living-In-Step   **35**

Four.   What's My Name?   **56**

Five.   Trading Spaces: Visitation   **72**

Six.   Christmas Comes But Once a Year: Annual Events   **95**

Seven.   Can We All Just Get Along?   **114**

Eight.   Love and Money   **125**

Nine.   Step Parenting Can Make You Sick   **141**

Ten.   The Kitchen Wars   **155**

Eleven. I Love Them, I Love Them Not   **167**

Twelve. The Path to Forgiveness   **177**

Thirteen.   Living, Loving, and Learning, One Step at a Time   **193**

Notes from the Author   **206**

Acknowledgements

To my husband - Thank you for being the love of my life and for sharing your children with me. Thank you for reminding me daily, that with God all things are possible.

To my biological children Austin and Addy - Thank you for being exceptional children despite my life choices. I am forever grateful for your unconditional love and devotion.

To my stepchildren – Braxton, Jasmine, Jacqulyn, Bobby, Jr., Benjamin, and Brian - Thank you for allowing me to be a part of your lives and for sharing your father with me.

My spiritual team – The Second Baptist Church Women's Bible study group and my prayer partner Carol Dietzschold –Your prayer circles kept me focused and encouraged.

To my siblings and parents – Thanks for allowing me to work during family events and for your continued love and support.

To my proof readers -.Luttra Lewis, Bettie Young, and Beverly White – I am appreciative of your tireless efforts. Thank you for your helping to make my vision a reality.

To my editor, Adele Brinkley - You are invaluable; I have learned immensely from your wisdom.

 To my publisher, Dr. A'ndrea J. Wilson and Divine Garden Press – I am so blessed to have a thorough and supportive publisher. You are the best! Thank you for allowing me to contribute to your vision to "save marriages one book at a time."

To my readers and fellow stepmoms – Thank you for reading One Plus One Equals Ten: A Survival Guide for Stepmoms. Now unto him that is able to do exceedingly abundantly above all that we ask or think, according to the power that worketh in us (Ephesians 3:20 KJV).

Janice

To my husband Bobby, who has continued to love me in spite of who I am. Your love inspires me to do great things.
Thank you for believing in me.

Foreword

It was not until I became "one of them" that I developed an appreciation and heightened sensitivity to the need of a new ministry that had not yet unfolded in my life. With over two decades of Christian ministry under my belt, I thought I had a handle on what families were going through when there is a divorce and/or a remarriage, and families with children are forced to join together. What I soon discovered was an up close and very personal reality check that exposed the truth of how admittedly wrong I was.

In church life in any town U.S.A., it is often the rule rather than the exception for church leaders and pastors alike to tell couples "just pray about it" (their circumstances) and the good Lord will work it out. Sounds too familiar, doesn't it? Perhaps you have uttered those same words yourself or were given them as advice for whatever ailed you. Well, a smidgen of the cliché is partially true; however, the part that is missing can be found in this book, as told through the personal voice of my courageous wife Janice.

Someone once said that families with children don't actually blend when remarriage happens; they just collide. It was not until I became one of them, a divorced father with six children who married a divorced mother with two children, that I really understood stepfamily struggles. Then together, Janice and I prayed for help! We were determined to survive the battles that usually destroy stepfamilies and live to tell the story first hand. Every morning we prayed together and asked the Lord to let our lives be a blessing to someone else by word or deed.

This work was actually born out of the depths of a praying woman who did not have a clue as to what she was getting into as she entered my complicated world. But I must admit; I am so glad that she did not know! This is our story. It is a real life story that illuminates the perilous pitfalls lying in wait to wreck your family. Janice is uniquely qualified to share her perspective as a woman who walks the walk each and every day, as a pastor's wife, mother, stepmother, grandmother, and professional. She talks the talk–straight talk and holds nothing back. I am confidently sure as you read these pages, you will begin to see what she saw and identify with the emotions, hurt feelings, and sheer frustrations that occur in everyday stepfamily relationships where everybody is trying to do the best they can to make it work. Janice shares essential Biblical references that will provide you with the hope genuinely needed to assist you in making the best of your family's journey.

Thank you, Janice, for your courage and your continued faith in God. Thank you for your willingness to share and your passion and desire to help others. Most of all, thank you for being my wife.

Rev. Dr. Bobby L. Love, Sr.
Pastor, Second Baptist Church of Olathe

Introduction

This is my life's work; helping people understand and respond to this message. It came as a sheer gift to me, a real surprise; God handling all the details. I was the least qualified of any available Christians. God saw to it that I was equipped, but you can be sure it had nothing to do with my natural abilities. And so here I am, preaching and writing about things that are way over my head, the inexhaustible riches and generosity of Christ.
Ephesians 3: 7-11 (The Message)

I opened my eyes to find him holding a stunning marquis diamond ring and asking me to be his wife. Was I imagining things? Did Rev. Bobby Love, the pastor of my church, just ask me to marry him? We were merely sitting there, talking about work and other things when he asked me to close my eyes. Time stood still, the moment was picture perfect. We had been dating for only three months, and the last thing I was expecting was a marriage proposal. Before I knew it, "yes" automatically came out of my mouth. He slipped the ring on my finger, and I gave him the biggest hug and kiss ever. Oh my God, we were going to be married! Once, the immediate excitement wore off, I asked the all-important question, "So when should we get married?"

He joyfully responded, "What are you doing New Year's Eve?" Even though it was the last week in November, I let him convince me to get married on New Year's Day. We would marry during the first month, on the first day of the year, at 1:00 p.m. at our church where he had served as senior pastor for over thirteen years.

As I sat there admiring the sparkling engagement ring and mirroring the enormous smile on his face, suddenly it hit me: I had just agreed to marry a man with six kids! I had two of my own! Had I lost my mind? That's a total of eight kids! We would be a family of ten people! Visions of driving the church van to get all of us to church, flashed before me. What happened to the perfect life I had planned for myself, being married once, having two children, and living happily ever after? I would have never thought I would be divorced, be single again, remarry, and then become a stepmom, much less to six children. I was about to ruin the moment when I looked into Bobby's eyes and realized only God could have brought us both through very trying times and blessed us to find one another. "Okay, New Year's Day it is," I said, trying to hide my inner thoughts.

Later in the evening, Bobby and I discussed how the church and our children would respond to our decision to marry. Initially, we had more anxiety about the reaction of the congregation. Concerning our children, we were optimistic because although both of our previous marriages had failed, Bobby and I were great parents and had remarkable kids. We loved each other, so surely our kids would feel the same way. Therefore, we convinced ourselves that once married, we would have a few issues related to bringing our families together. Everything was going to be bright and sunny. The Love family would have a smooth, fast, transition. What's more, we had the Lord on our side. Where could we go wrong? Our short time dating was splendid. Our kids enjoyed playing together, and his kids adored me as their youth teacher. Life was going to be wonderful! We could demonstrate our solidarity by including all of our children in the wedding.

We were so in love. All of our plans were coming together nicely until two weeks before the wedding when two of Bobby's children decided it would be best if they didn't attend our nuptials. We were disappointed, but not deterred because six out of eight of our children were still planning to attend and/or participate. The final weekend prior to our big day, we slightly reorganized my house to move

Bobby's belongings in and made the necessary adjustments to accommodate five children on alternating weekends. It wasn't optimal, but we could definitely make this work until we could afford to purchase something more suitable for our new stepfamily.

We had a beautiful wedding, making us an officially a stepfamily. Six out of eight of our children did attend and much of our family was there to support us. A day later was our first opportunity to sleep under one roof with all of our minor children. Night one, we discovered a hiccup. We were used to much different sleeping environments. I and mine liked it dark and quiet, Bobby and his wanted lights and noise. Unexpectedly, we arose the next morning with our first reality; this union may not be as unproblematic as we thought.

As a wedding gift, our neighbors, who were also a stepfamily, gave us a book called *Living in a Stepfamily without Getting Stepped On*. I placed the book on the bookshelf and decided we really didn't need it, but as we began to experience stepfamily conflict, I deliberately searched for answers. I located the stored away book, but discovered it didn't have the solutions I was looking for. On my next trip to the library, I checked out any printed material available on stepfamilies. As I frequented bookstores, I accumulated every book I could find. There were additional books found on Amazon and a few stepfamily websites. Each writer approached the subject differently, and I was able to find helpful guidelines for some support. Because we were Christians and church leaders, we wanted a Biblical perspective. Surely there were some Christian resources out there for stepfamilies. After all, Jesus was raised by a man who wasn't his father, and so was Moses. I discovered fewer resources were available to give godly advice on how to live victoriously in a stepfamily.

Reaching desperation, I also sought the advice of other families who I knew had gone through similar situations. Some counsel was beneficial, yet we continued to struggle. There were some highs and then some extreme lows to the point I almost regretted getting married. To relieve stress, I began to journal my experiences, thoughts, and emotions, all of which eventually led to the writing of this book. Therefore, know that this is a personal perspective on what we experienced as a stepfamily. These words include the adventures of my life when I made the decision to marry a man with six children. It is amusing as I see the shock on women's faces and hear them mutter, "He must be some kind of man," or "You must really love him." All the above are true; I married an absolutely wonderful and adoring man, who loves me unconditionally, and whom God designed just for me.

Before I offer my insight, let me make one thing perfectly clear. Stepfamilies are not like biological families and will never operate as biological families do. I know your assumption is that you will love your stepchildren the same way you love your biological children. This assumption is a myth that can possibly destroy your spirit and your marriage. Loving them the same way you love your own children is not possible, but it does not mean you can't develop a deliberate and special kind of love for stepchildren that works for your family. Once you understand the dynamics of living-in-step and learn to manage your everyday lives, your family can be successful.

Our adventures were such a shock for me that I had to caution others considering going down this road. After we had been married for five years, we sought professional help to understand the dynamics of stepfamilies by attending training at the Stepfamily Foundation. My husband, who is a Christian counselor, became a Certified Stepfamily Counselor, and I became a Certified Stepfamily Coach. While preparing for the certification workshop, I came across a startling statistic that really frightened me. "Of those women who marry men with children, 85% of them are career women. Of those career women who married men with children, 65% of them said that that if they had to do it over again, they would never marry a man with children and become a stepmother. Hmmmmm . . .

As we were really going through our struggles, I couldn't help but agree with the sixty-five percent; however, I was committed to my marriage and had finally met the man of my dreams, my soul mate, the man God had placed on earth just for me. Even though it was considered, another divorce was not an option for me. I was trying to be the woman God called me to be.

As I tell our story, I am protective of our family; therefore, all of our children have been given fictitious names which they selected themselves. My children are Aaron and Aiden, and Bobby's children are Bryson, Brody, Janae, Brayden, Jamie, and Brandon. Despite the fact that friends and family can identify everyone, my goal is to share our story without causing hurt or harm to our family unit. Using our personal journey as an example will hopefully illustrate the challenges of living-in-step. When I shared with others that I was writing a book, I was asked if I could be transparent. I realized the necessity to be so if we were going to be able to help someone else.

At the conclusion of each chapter are "Stepmom Survival Tips," which are my suggestions or helpful tips for those of you living-in-step. Helpful scriptures are also provided to meditate and pray about. Please review the stepmom tips and helpful scriptures, and then spend time discussing them and praying with your spouse and or other stepmoms.

We are still praying and working to become the family God has called us to be. Hopefully as you read our stories, you will find yourself, laughing, crying, agreeing, and sometimes disagreeing on how we handled our situations and the choices we made. We pray you will be encouraged and blessed living, loving and learning in-step!

Chapter One
Dating With Children

There are three or four things I cannot understand: How eagles fly so high or snakes crawl on rocks, how ships sail the ocean or people fall in love.
Proverbs 30:18-20 (CEV)

Four years after my divorce, dating was the last thing on my mind. The divorce process had been difficult for my children and me, but life was going considerably well. We had made a new home for ourselves in the small community of Olathe, Kansas. The kids enjoyed their new schools and had adjusted well. My son Aaron (15) was seven years older than his sister Aiden (8); therefore, he could babysit her whenever needed. I had a wonderful support system, including other single women I had met at church through the singles ministry. Every other weekend when my children went to visit their father, there was time to travel, catch up on work, hang out with girlfriends, be lazy, or do whatever I wanted to do.

Since my divorce, I had been in contact with a few men from past college relationships and had met a few new ones; however, I did not consider myself in the market for a boyfriend or a husband. Many friends and acquaintances had approached me about being set up on a blind date with someone they knew who was perfect for me, but I just didn't feel like accepting any offers. A few guys at church showed interest, but I was not interested in dating. Life was good without a mate, and I considered myself "single and satisfied."

At church, I was involved in several activities which involved working with youth. Also, I was a dedicated member of the singles ministry and often spent time encouraging others to stay focused on their goals rather than expending their energy looking for a mate. My consistent message to the never married was to make sure they found the right person before taking the marital plunge.

The Lord and I Can Take Care of Us

One of the major difficulties of divorce is the financial strain that occurs for both persons once separated. When my former husband and I divorced, we were making roughly the same amount of money, so I didn't receive alimony, and the child support I received was what I would call average. Because I wanted to maintain a "Johnson County" standard of living, more income was needed for our household. I was blessed to find a higher paying job, and my career with a community health center provided the financial support needed for my family. I was fortunate also to purchase a four bedroom home with schools in walking distance. There was a nice size yard for the kids to play in, plus a two car garage to store my extra belongings.

I did my best to manage money wisely and all of my bills were current. Spending was not extravagant even though I had splurged on a vacation one year and taken my kids to Cancun for spring break. I was paying tithes at church and therefore, living a blessed life. My confidence and trust was in God who provided well for us.

My mother, by default, had taught me never to depend on a man to support me. I did not need a man for financial reasons and didn't feel like I needed one for emotional reasons either. I was not praying for a husband or even a boyfriend as some of my friends were. Oddly, one Easter I was approached by a gentleman at church who asked if I would like for him to purchase Easter outfits for my children. I think he was trying to impress me. I was obviously offended and wanted to tell him what he could do with his money and himself. However, because I was at church, I curtly stated, "I can take care of me and my children."

When You Least Expect It

The following statement had proven true for many of my single girlfriends and me: "When you are looking for a man, you can't find one." At the same time, when we weren't looking, prospects seemed to come out of nowhere, and I never imagined I would be dating the pastor of my church. I had my reasons, including the fact my former husband was a pastor, and I did not desire to once again have my private life become the headlines of the church society page. Somehow, he asked me out me out to dinner before I had time to rationalize the many valid reasons as to why I shouldn't go on a date with the pastor of my church, the Reverend Bobby Love, Sr.

He was a divorced pastor with six children, and he and his family were widely known in our small community. At the very top of the list was the fact he had experienced a highly public, devastating divorce that almost ruined him. As a result of the divorce, he had suffered emotionally in the previous year, including having to get a vote of confidence from his congregation to remain the pastor of the Second Baptist Church of Olathe, Kansas. Worst of all he was a Republican interested in running for office!

However, despite the speculations about what had happened to his marriage of twenty years, he had been an effective pastor for over thirteen years. He was known as a community leader who was committed to serving others. Notwithstanding his looming issues, to his credit, he was tall, dark, and handsome with sad puppy dog eyes. Rev. Bobby Love was intelligent, a wonderful conversationalist with a great sense of humor, and he possessed qualities that soon gained my attention. Before I get ahead of myself, let me tell you how we ended up on a date in the first place.

Best Girlfriends

It's a blessing to have good friends. Tina is a very special friend of mine. After joining Second Baptist Church, I immediately noticed she was one who loved to dress "Baptist style" by wearing church hats. Being a former pastor's wife, my closet included a fine assortment of fashionable hats which I had no plans of wearing again. One of my favorites was navy blue with feathers and rhinestones, which was a little too large for my head. One Sunday, I decided to take it to Tina because I knew she would look great in it. She appreciated the gesture, and the next week she brought me an adorable purse from her cousin's boutique in California. We instantly became the best of friends and have remained so ever since.

We enjoyed many of the same things and often went to movies, dinner, and each other's house. Tina was the only person in Kansas I had introduced to my family who lived in Oklahoma. My mom and sisters loved meeting her and adopted her into our family. Also, her granddaughter was my daughter's best friend, so we often attended events as a foursome. On a few occasions when I had to travel, she kindly stayed at my house and took care of my children.

Tina has the gift of hospitality and often takes care of those who are among her friends and family, including her church family. She had raised her own kids, adopted two others, and everybody in the community calls her Aunt Tina. Tina was definitely my best friend in the area. She was not only a blessing to me, but also many others in our church and neighborhood. After church on Sundays, any number of people would gather at her house to enjoy one of Tina's famous Sunday meals, complete with greens, cornbread, and her famous macaroni and cheese and potato salad.

Friends and Fellowship

One hot Tuesday evening in early August 2002, our church was hosting our district's annual business session. Pastor Love was the esteemed moderator of our district, and it was the occasion for him to deliver his annual address. Because Second Baptist was hosting the event, the members had been encouraged to attend what was referred to as Moderator's Night. I considered myself a dedicated member of the church and wanted to be supportive of the program; therefore, I decided to attend the evening service. Having never attended a district function, I didn't know what to expect. We were told to be there around 6:30 Tuesday evening.

I got off work at 5:30 PM, picked up my daughter, purchased food for the kids, ran home, and changed into something appropriate for church. Being rushed, I didn't bother to eat and hurried off to church, arriving there around 6:45 PM. As soon as I arrived, I realized the district session wasn't an ordinary church service. The good news, however, was that Pastor Love hadn't started preaching yet. After thirty minutes of other people speaking about things I didn't understand, the choir moved to the choir stand and sang a few songs, after which Pastor Love delivered an inspiring message on how he had led the district.

Following the service, I was heading out the door when my friend Tina stopped me and asked if I had eaten dinner. Because I was hungry, we decided to pick up Chinese take-out. Not wanting to take two cars, and with the restaurant being only five blocks away, she hopped into my car. Twenty minutes later when we returned to pick up her car, Pastor Love's car and hers were the only cars left in the parking lot. We really weren't concerned about his car being there because Tina indicated it was not unusual for him to be at the church late in the evening. However, he had thought it strange to see her car still in the parking lot on a weekday night and decided to finish up a few miscellaneous items and wait to see if she was going to return to pick up her car.

When we arrived back in the parking lot, Pastor Love walked out of his office and headed towards my car to ask if everything was okay. We assured him everything was fine, telling him that we had just gone to pick up some food and were leaving. Tina, being the caretaker she is known for, asked him if he had eaten dinner. When he said no, she quickly invited him over to her house to join us. She assured him we had enough food to share. Rev. Love was hungry and knew Tina's home was a safe haven for him, so he agreed to join us.

When he walked away from the car, I asked her why on earth she would invite him to her house at 9:00 o'clock on a Tuesday night. I argued with her quietly and objected because I didn't want to be caught dead or alive anywhere near Pastor Love. There were about five hundred rumors going around about him and women within the church, and I didn't want my name coming up in any of them. After objecting about five times, she finally convinced me to stick with the original plan to go to her house to eat. Our three cars headed to Tina's house, which was less than three minutes away from the church.

With the front door wide open, we gathered around Tina's dining room table eating Chinese food. We shared food and laughed about everything under the sun. The conversation included dream travel destinations, our favorite cities, our favorite restaurants and foods, our favorite neighborhoods, our dream houses and any other subject that came to mind. Before long, Rev. Love and I realized we had a lot of things in common, and it seemed as though we enjoyed many of the same things. I couldn't believe it. We were actually engaged in a really great conversation. I hadn't enjoyed a conversation with a man in a long time. I almost forgot he was my pastor. Even Tina found herself looking back and forth at the two of us and saying, "Wow, you two like the same things."

The subject changed, and we began to talk about all of the turmoil the church had experienced when Rev. Love divorced and how innocent people had been hurt by all the rumors. Many single women who were members had been accused of having a relationship with the newly single pastor. Tina and I had discussed in previous conversations that both of our names had come up as possible candidates for consideration. Church gossip was one of the main reasons I didn't want to be seen anywhere near Rev. Love. I knew the rumors would start to surface immediately. I had lived a quiet life since moving to Olathe and didn't want any trouble for myself or my children. I especially didn't want to be part of any church scandal.

He continued discussing how many single women had suffered distress because of his situation. Knowing my name had been brought up in the gossip that surrounded his personal affairs, Rev. Love offered an apology for any heartache I may have experienced being a single woman in his church. His statement made me nervous, and I wasn't quite sure how to respond, so I sat quietly and nodded. The table was suddenly quiet. He broke the silence by smiling and stating that the imagined story regarding him and me was a compliment to him and wasn't such an awful idea. He then asked me if I would consider joining him for lunch sometime.

Fortune Cookies

After his lunch invitation, the conversation was no longer amusing, and I became extremely nervous. The last thing I expected was to be asked out on a date by this man. My first instinct was to say no, but I told him I would think about it. He then asked if he could at least call me because he really enjoyed our conversation. Nervously, I agreed to a phone call. He said, "Great, I will call you tomorrow."

After his statement of confirmation, I grew to be more nervous and jumped up to begin clearing the table in order to make a quick exit. I moved as fast as I could to get to the kitchen. Tina doesn't permit anyone to help her do much in the kitchen, whether it is cooking or cleaning, so she ran me out and told me to go back in there with the pastor. Amused at my behavior, she followed me back to the dining room.

In order to prepare for a quick escape, I reminded everyone of the time and that we all had to go to work the next day. After glancing at the clock, we decided to end the evening by opening our fortune cookies. Both Tina and I opened ours and found the traditional fortune cookie message, such as you will be rich and famous or a famous Chinese proverb. We read ours aloud and waited to see what his said. He stared at the small piece of paper in astonishment and started smiling, but did not seem interested in sharing his fortune with us. We inquired, but he shook his head no, continuing to grin.

We thought the behavior to be strange and were really curious about what was printed on his fortune cookie. After asking several times and threatening to snatch the paper out of his hand, he finally agreed to give it to Tina. Once she read it, her eyebrows raised in bewilderment. Now, I was really anxious to know what it said. I begged her to read it. Amazingly, the words printed on the fortune cookie read, "What you are looking for is right in front of you."

That's right you guessed it. Guess who was sitting right in front of him? Again, the room became quiet, and I was ready to faint! It was definitely time to go, so I said goodnight and practically ran out of the door. As I was on my way out of the door, Pastor Love followed me, indicating what a great time he had and reminded me he was going to call me tomorrow. I replied, "Okay, Pastor Love." He asked if I would call him Bobby. Now, I knew I was in trouble. I got out of there and made it home in record time.

Of course, I didn't get any sleep, wondering what on earth had happened and how I had gotten myself into such a situation. The worst part was, I could tell by the beaming smile on his face, he was definitely going to call very soon. I was hoping the call would not come before Wednesday night bible study, for I didn't know how I was going to be able to act normal around him. I was scared to death, but at the same time, I was intrigued. Our conversation had seemed so natural and fulfilling. Was it because I hadn't had an enjoyable conversation with a man in so long and I didn't know any better?

The following day I sent Tina an email and asked her if I had been "set up." She said, "No, but it was hilarious to watch miss always-has-herself-together acting so nervous." She then reminded me to stay out of her kitchen. Because she and Rev. Love worked in the same building, he had already stopped by to thank her for the invite and to tell her he had a new cookie favorite . . . fortune cookies!

Of course, Bobby called me the next day, then the next day, and so on and so forth, and since then not a day has gone by in which we have not had a conversation by phone. Most of our telephone conversations lasted at least two hours and were always wonderful and pleasurable.

Our First Date

Three weeks later, he convinced me to go on a date; it was August 25, 2002. We still celebrate this day annually. We agreed to meet for lunch at McCormick and Schmick's on the plaza because we both liked seafood and it was close to my office. Both of us were extremely nervous, so we were barely able to eat our food. As usual, the conversation was free flowing, but it was much better being face-to-face. After being at the restaurant for an hour or so, the lunch crowd began to dwindle. We were enjoying ourselves so much we didn't want to return to work, but I had some unfinished assignments so I knew our lunch had to come to an end. We agreed to go on another date the next weekend when I did not have my children.

Within a matter of weeks and before I realized it, the phone calls and dates were more frequent, and we were beginning to think of ourselves as a dating couple. I began referring to him as my boyfriend; however, I was still afraid to tell anyone outside of my immediate circle. I sought the advice of some godly women at my church and asked them how they felt about me dating the pastor. They asked questions, shared their wisdom, prayed with me, and encouraged me to follow my heart.

Bobby and I spent a lot of time together on weekends when my children were visiting their father. Our time seemed so short, and then it was time for him to go home. He wanted to spend more time with me so he asked if he could stop by some evenings after work. Even though I enjoyed his company, I did not want him to come to my house while the kids were there because I had not talked with them about him. Only a few of our closest friends knew we were dating, and we felt it would be best if it stayed that way for now. Because Bobby was the pastor of our church and I was a member who attended regularly, our brief conversations after church quickly became noticed and the buzz amongst members. A few nosey members had even driven by my house and seen his car parked in the driveway on Fridays and Saturdays when my children were away. Oddly, some even knew what time he often left at night. He usually left at a decent hour, for he was temporarily residing with his parents and didn't like waking them up too late. I still wanted to hold off on weekday visits, but I also knew I didn't want my kids to get the news from somewhere else.

Should We Include Our Children?

Having been divorced for several years, my children were aware I had gone on a few casual dates from time to time. However, if I went on a date, it was usually the weekends that they were not at home. I don't think they were opposed to me dating, but we had never really discussed the topic. Some divorce data suggest children are at least two years emotionally behind their parents when it comes to divorce. By the time the divorce actually happens, the adult is already adjusting emotionally and wanting to complete the process. On the other hand, children may believe the divorce is not going to happen or not aware of how their lives will be affected. After two years, the adult may be ready to move on and begin dating, but the children are just making the transition and adjustment to their new lives. I remember sometime after my ex-husband and I divorced, the kids and I were house hunting. While touring the master bedroom, my daughter asked me the strangest question. "Is that where you and daddy are going to sleep?" I had to break her heart by telling her daddy would continue to live in his apartment, and we were the only ones who were going to be living in our new house.

Some children of divorce are still hanging on to the belief and desire that their parents will get back together. A movie my daughter and I often watched together is entitled *Parent Trap*, in which a divorced couple reunites because of their daughters' intervention. By the end of the movie, the adults see life and love the kids' way and magically decide they want to be married again. They even manage to run off the fiancé' of their father, so they don't end up with a wicked stepmom. Another movie favorite of hers at the time was *House Arrest*, where the children locked their parents in the basement until they agreed to work things out and stay married.

Neither one of us had any intentions of reuniting with our former spouses. My children had been given plenty of time to adjust because I had been divorced for approximately four years when Bobby and I begin to date. On the other hand, Bobby's children may still have been of the belief that their parents could get back together and had not even thought about their parents dating. Because the news of our dating was spreading quickly, we knew it was time to have some discussions with our children.

Guess Who's Coming to Dinner?

The Labor Day holiday sounded like a perfect opportunity to invite Bobby over for dinner when I knew my children would be home and relaxed. Early in the day, as I was preparing the grill, I informed my children that Pastor Love was coming over for dinner. Aaron, who was fifteen years old at the time, responded by asking the question, "What's he coming over here for? Does he like you or something?"

I said, "Yes, he is interested in dating me."

Because his father was a minister, Aaron's response was "What is it with you and preachers?"

I responded, "I guess it's something written on my forehead." Aiden didn't say anything. I finished grilling, cleaned up the house, and got dressed for our dinner guest. Soon Bobby's white Cadillac pulled up in the driveway, and the doorbell rang. The kids stayed in their rooms until I asked them to come down for dinner.

Before dinner was served, Bobby and I discussed whether or not we would sit at the dining room table or be more informal and eat in the den. Because my kids were used to seeing me sit at the head of the dining room table, we decided to be more casual and eat in the den. I called the kids down, and everyone exchanged pleasantries. We blessed the food, and everyone served themselves. Aaron ate at the breakfast bar, and Aiden surprisingly came downstairs and asked if she could eat with us. We excitedly said yes! Aiden was usually pretty shy around most people, so it was a surprise to Bobby to hear her actually talk. She stayed down in the den with us until she finished her meal and then she went back up to her room. Aaron came down for a little while to talk about school, sports, and so forth.

Bobby stayed until around 10:00 PM, and after he left, my children didn't ask any questions about his visit. After that day, Bobby began to visit on a regular basis. The kids began to expect his daily visits after I got home from work. Bobby is a coffee connoisseur and drinks coffee all hours of the day. I owned a coffee pot, but wasn't a coffee drinker, so I had to dig through boxes in the basement to find the small coffee maker. Whenever he came over, I prepared a pot of coffee, so the aroma soon became the signal that Bobby was coming over. One evening, he was running a few hours late, and Aaron asked, "Are you not making any coffee tonight?" His question let me know my kids expected Bobby's regular visits.

Daddy, Do You Have a Girlfriend?

Bobby experienced something much different when he began to have conversations with his children about dating me. By the time he spoke with them, they were already aware of our relationship, for their mother had informed them. He was asked very boldly by one of his children whether or not we were dating and why he wanted to go out with anyone. He acknowledged we were dating and said he would be spending more and more time with me. This report caused a variety of emotions and responses from his children. The younger ones were excited to hear that their father had a girlfriend, and the older ones had assumed it would happen sooner or later. It was the "who" that disturbed the older ones the most. Bobby found himself suddenly assuming a defensive posture, answering question after question about why he chosen me to go out with. He talked with the younger children about how nice I was and how much fun he and I had together. The dominating question on their minds was whether or not we were going to get married. Bobby didn't answer the question.

Bobby's oldest son Bryson (24) was a true fan of mine and was excited to hear we were dating. His joyful response was, "She is really a neat lady." On the other hand his other two adult children, Brody (20) and Janae (19), disapproved and were very vocal about their emotions. They openly expressed their disappointment in their father and wanted to know why he would even think about dating someone they knew. After all, I was their Sunday school teacher and they liked me; now they would have to look at me differently. Bobby's children had always enjoyed having me as the teacher for the youth department and enjoyed being in my classes. Our children were familiar with one another, had participated in activities together, and gotten along well.

Bobby and I had the same weekend visitation schedule. On "kid weekends," as we called them, we spent time with our own children and dated only on the weekends when we had no children. As our relationship grew more serious, we wanted to see one another on the weekends when we had our children. One Friday, we planned a get together and decided he would bring his kids over to my house. Friday nights at my house were Pizza Hut nights. After a long week at work, I refused to cook, and besides, the kids loved pizza. Bobby agreed to swing by and pick up the pizza. Bobby brought along with him the younger boys, Brayden (12) and Brandon (7).

At first, everyone was a little shy as we ate pizza, but afterwards, the kids retreated to the bedrooms to play. They had a great time playing together just as they had done in the past. We were fortunate Bobby's son Brayden was three years younger than my son Aaron, and looked up to him as being a "cool guy." Aiden was two years older than Brandon, but nonetheless, they were great playmates. They played video games and with any other toys she had in her room. They played and watched television and peaked in on us every now and then. We sat back on the couch, watched television, and thought "this isn't so bad." Everyone had a great time, so we figured we would do this every kid weekend. This practice continued each weekend we had our children.

Bobby's youngest daughter, Jamie (9), had not made any of the previous visits because she did not always visit Bobby on visitation weekends. She had heard from her brothers that they had been over for several visits and she was bubbling with curiosity. We really desired to include her in a visit also. On the evening she came along, she needed to have her hair washed. I wasn't a beautician, but I had become pretty good at washing and styling Aiden's hair, so I offered to do her hair as a favor to Bobby. I did so, and she appreciated my hard work. She also had fun, and from that point on we began spending every Friday evening entertaining one another whether we had the kids or not. Bobby did meet some resistance from the children's mother for his children spending a lot of time at my house; however, we continued to spend time together every weekend.

All Things Work Together for Good

Bobby and I spent a lot of time discussing what had gone wrong in our first marriages. I had been divorced for four years and had minimal emotions and issues remaining from the marriage and the divorce. Bobby's divorce was a long drawn out process, and even though they had been separated for some time prior to the divorce, they had only been legally divorced only four months before we started dating. Their life was still pretty much in turmoil. He and his ex-wife were still arguing regularly. His children were still asking the question, why their parent's had divorced, and were convinced their lives were ruined forever. Everyone was disoriented and our dating only made the situation with the children and their mother worse. Church life was also a challenge for Bobby, for the church was adjusting to him being divorced, and now they had to accept the idea he was dating. I requested prayer from several people to pray for everyone's best interest. It was definitely a miracle God had brought us together. We both believed Romans 8:28 that promises us that all things work together for good.

Even though our dating was now very public and the topic of many conversations, it was an exciting time for Bobby and me. We enjoyed getting to know one another and desired to spend as much time as possible in one another's presence or talking on the phone. On weekdays, after Bobby left my house and went home, we would call each other and continue our conversation until midnight. We soon learned we could fight our battles better together than apart. A few months went by and before we realized it, Bobby had proposed, and we had made the decision to become one. We still had a lot to pray about and to prepare for, mostly related to the church and our children. Our prayer was for our church and Bobby's ministry to be blessed because of our future union. I was looking forward to supporting him in every way I could to help our church to heal from the wounds of the past. Our prayer for our children was that they too would be blessed and that their lives would be enhanced and healed. I was excited about supporting Bobby as a father and a new stepfather. I knew he would encourage me as a mother and a stepmother. Everything was going to work out in our favor. Right?

Stepmom Survival Tips

1. Pray and seek the advice of godly counsel before making any decisions about your future.
2. Don't date too soon after ending a marriage. Wait at least a year. Two years is optimal.
3. Make sure children have had enough time to adjust to your divorce or relationship ending.
4. Introduce your children to your date only if you are serious about the relationship.
5. If the relationship is leading toward marriage, inform the ex-spouse of your plans.
6. When introducing or being introduced to the children, plan a fun outing in a neutral setting.
7. Plan regular date outings with and without the children.
8. Have conversations about marriage, divorce, and relationships with your children based on their ages. Allow them to express their feelings.
9. Reassure children they will not be deserted because of your dating relationship.
10. It is best not to allow a date to spend the night in the presence of your children. If it is unavoidable, sleep in separate quarters.

Helpful Scriptures

Psalm 112: 1-2 (NIV)
Blessed are those who fear the Lord, who find great delight in his commands. Their children will be mighty in the land; the generation of the upright will be blessed.

Psalm 73:25-26 (NIV)
Whom have I in heaven but you? And earth has nothing I desire besides you. My flesh and my heart may fail, but God is the strength of my heart and my portion forever.

I Thessalonians 4:3-5 (NKJV)
For it is the will of God, your sanctification: that you should abstain from sexual immorality; that each of you should know how to possess his own vessel in sanctification and honor, not in passion of lust, like the Gentiles who do not know God.

Jeremiah 29:11 (NIV)
"For I know the plans I have for you," declares the Lord, "plans to prosper you and not harm you, plans to give you a hope and a future".

Romans 8:28 (KJV)
And we know that all things work together for good to them that love God, to them who are the called according to his purpose.

Chapter Two
One Big Happy Stepfamily

The priest answered them, "Go in peace. Your journey has the Lord's approval." Judges 18:6 (NIV)

The Proposal

While dating, Bobby and I had discussed marriage briefly, but the formal proposal came the Wednesday after Thanksgiving. He called me mid-morning and asked if I was available for lunch. I wasn't planning to take time for lunch, but he wouldn't take no for an answer, so I had to move some appointments around on my calendar. We met at the Capitol Grille on the plaza and sat in the famous Count Basie booth. While we were eating, Bobby seemed distracted and nervous, but excited about something. After we finished the meal, and the wait staff cleared the table, Bobby got really quiet, which was unusual for him. He then asked me to close my eyes. I did as he asked, and when I opened my eyes, he proposed with a beautiful marquis diamond engagement ring.

I guess by now you know I said yes, as I tried to hold back the tears. He explained how he had worked with his jeweler to design the gorgeous ring and hoped I would appreciate his choice. Not long after placing the ring on my finger, I realized we were really talking about getting married! I went back to work eager to tell the world we were going to be married and ecstatic to show off my stunning engagement ring.

Later in the evening, we discussed wedding plans and decided there was no need to have an extended engagement period. We selected January 1, 2003, New Year's Day as our official wedding date. What a way to start off the year. Our new life together would begin on the first day of the year at one o'clock hour in the afternoon. The ceremony would be held at our church.

Six weeks seemed like plenty of time to tell our families so they could plan their holiday schedules accordingly. All of my immediate family was coming from Oklahoma or Texas, and my Uncle David and Aunt Jane were coming from as far as New Jersey. Most of Bobby's immediate family was in Kansas and wouldn't require a flight to attend. As long as the weather was good, most of them would be able to drive to the Kansas City area.

There were so many decisions to make. I had to find a dress, decide who was going to be in the wedding, prepare the children, and a million other things. Soon, I wondered how I let Bobby talk me into New Year's Day. Because thanksgiving had already passed, holiday shopping had begun, and most of the stores were crammed with holiday shoppers. I rationalized with myself the less time I had to plan, the less money I would spend. The wedding would be simple, yet elegant.

The Big Announcement

We first told our parents and then brothers and sisters, close friends, other family, and then our children about our engagement and plan to be married. The announcement did not surprise our children, and for the most part, some of them appeared to be excited. The question plaguing the younger one's minds was if they were going to be in the wedding. We assured them if they wanted to participate, they could. Because our guest list was short and consisted mostly of close family and friends, we decided to do verbal invitations instead of printed

One Plus One Equals Ten

ones. Mostly, we would invite only those persons who had been encouraging towards us concerning our dating relationship.

During the morning worship service on the first Sunday in December, Bobby asked me to stand before the church congregation. He then announced from the pulpit, we were engaged and planning to be married. He intentionally did not give the date. I could tell he was nervous because we didn't know how our members would react. Members responded with a variety of emotions. Following the morning service, I can count on two hands the number of church members who congratulated me or approached me regarding the announcement. I was disheartened to notice several members who were usually friendly towards me, didn't even bother to speak. Those who showed their support on that day were added to our guest list.

Once our engagement was announced, I could publicly make plans for our simple, yet elegant wedding. Because it was winter, I chose colors that gave me the sensation of warmth; champagne and black velvet. My friend Tina agreed to be my maid of honor, and we selected a lovely black velvet dress for her. For Aiden and Jamie, we found matching champagne and black dresses. All of the men participating in the ceremony owned tuxedos or black suits, and I located some great ties and cummerbunds to rent from a bridal shop. Our church decorator, Nette, surprised us and supplied an arch, candle stands, and other wedding decorations. My sister-in-law, Glendola, agreed to make the flowers.

In place of a traditional reception, we decided on a New Year's dinner for family and friends following the ceremony. Although we needed much more than luck, dinner, of course, would include black-eyed peas. We also decided to do a larger reception after we returned from our honeymoon for those who we did not invite to the wedding ceremony as a second opportunity to show support for our union.

A Family Affair

We began having conversations with our families about their attendance and participation in the wedding festivities. It was important to both of us that we have the support of our immediate families, particularly our children, parents, and siblings. Both of my children agreed to be a part of the ceremony. My mom was happy for us, so she wanted to partake. My dad chose not to take part for a couple reasons. The first reason was my dad's "one wedding tuxedo per daughter rule," which he established when my oldest sister got married. He wasn't fond of dressing up, but agreed to rent a tuxedo when each of his four daughters married. Because all of us daughters had married at least once, he had fulfilled his promise to dress appropriately for our weddings. When one of my sisters divorced and remarried, he did not give her away again; in fact, he did not even attend the wedding. He was not going to do anything special for my second wedding either. As soon as I confirmed my dad wasn't coming, I called my brother Tony who lives in Maryland and asked if he would do the honors. He was excited, as well as my three sisters who planned to attend along with their families.

Bobby's father was ecstatic and couldn't wait to go out and purchase a new suit for the big day. His mother had mixed emotions and wasn't sure how involved she wanted to be in the planning process or the wedding. Aware of her concerns, I spent some time alone with her so we could get to know one another better. During our conversation, I asked her personally if she would participate in the wedding. She agreed, and we spent the following Saturday shopping for a formal dress for her. Three of Bobby's four brothers did not live in the area, so they were not going to attend. One of his brothers lived locally and made plans to be present.

Bobby's oldest son Bryson was an amateur singer and wanted to participate by dedicating a song to us. Because we already had our singers and musicians selected and booked, we requested a song for our reception. Bobby's next oldest adult children, Brody and Janae, informed him privately they did not want to participate and weren't sure if they would attend. His youngest three wanted to be involved. Everything seemed to be moving along well as the date approached, and so far there had not been any major hiccups. However, two weeks before the wedding, Brayden decided he no longer wanted to participate. Janae decided it best if she did not attend. We didn't push either of them and guessed they most likely did not want to offend their mother. Bobby assured them we were okay with their decision.

During the planning stages, I spoke with my ex-husband and informed him of our plans. He gave his blessing and offered his support for caring for Aaron and Aiden while we went on our honeymoon. He also disclosed that he had received a call from one of our church members, asking him what he was going to do about Bobby and me getting married. The nerve of some people! He assured me that he had expressed to them to mind their own business and not to call his house again. I was grateful for his support.

Bobby did not have the courage to call his children's mother, so I called her regarding the children's participation in the wedding. She was disturbed that we had asked them to take part and felt as if we had bribed them by displaying the clothing we had selected for them for the ceremony. Her overall apprehension was that the children would grow up and regret we had tricked them into participating. Following my conversation with her, Bobby had additional discussions with each of them. In the end, Jamie and Brandon still wanted to participate. Regardless of how many of our eight children agreed to participate or attend, we were going to move forward with our plans.

The Rest of the Details

A huge concern for us was who would perform our ceremony. We prayed for direction. Being a widely known pastor in our community, Bobby knew many people who could conduct the wedding, but because of our complicated circumstances we wanted God's guidance to lead us to the right person. We discussed several pastors and finally decided that Rev. Otis Crawford from Chanute, Kansas, would be our choice. He and Bobby worked closely together as the leaders of our district association. Bobby called him and made the request, and he agreed to meet with us the following weekend. We spent some time with him and shared our unique story and asked if he would perform the ceremony for us. He was delighted and consented. He and his wife Ruby would make plans to arrive New Year's Eve. We informed him we would gladly take care of their hotel accommodations.

To put the ceremonial program together, I researched remarriages and second weddings to see what others had done. I reviewed Christian websites and books looking for information on proper etiquette for second marriages. First time brides have a variety of resources to assist with wedding plans; some were appropriate and useful, but I felt more comfortable with information I found for second time brides. It was important to both of us that our families be a part of the ceremony. We also wanted to make sure the vows and dedications were appropriate.

Based on our conversations, six out of eight of our children would attend, however, only five wanted to participate. Bobby's oldest son made plans to attend the wedding and sing at our reception. My son Aaron would assist my brother in giving me away by meeting us midway down the aisle. He would also double as an usher to light candles before the ceremony along with my nephew Willie. My daughter Aiden would be a flower girl along with Bobby's youngest daughter Jamie. The official ring bearer was to be Bobby's youngest son Brandon. I was thankful for Bobby's church secretary Angie, one of the few people excited about our wedding, for kindly putting the programs together complete with pictures. Her husband Jay agreed to be our professional photographer.

Christmas had come and gone, and my family began to arrive in town. My brother Tony's flight was delayed, and his luggage (with

the flowers in it) was lost. I was glad to see him when he finally
arrived and relieved when his suitcase arrived the following morning.
My Aunt Jane and Uncle David had flown in from New Jersey, and all
of my sisters and my mom arrived in Kansas. Bobby impressed my
whole family by preparing ribs on the grill. The night before the
wedding, my three sisters kept Bobby sequestered in a bedroom for
several hours, asking him a million questions. There had not been
enough time for them to get to know him during our short dating and
engagement period. They were eager to learn as much as possible in
one night about their future brother-in-law. After spending a few
hours with him, they gave me their full approval. Bobby was relieved
to get out that room in one piece.

Our Wedding Day

Finally, New Year's Day arrived, and we woke up to a cold, slightly
rainy, January day. Although we were up late seeing the New Year
come in, I was too excited to attempt sleeping late. I was up early
doing hair, making sure everyone could take a hot shower, and taking
care of last minute preparations. Bobby picked up Jamie and brought
her over for me to style her hair and help her dress. Bobby made sure
his youngest son Brandon had everything he needed. Time went by
quickly, and before we knew it, it was time to go to the church.

Because we verbally invited guests and did not ask for an RSVP,
we had no idea of how many people to expect. About seventy five
people were in attendance to witness our union. There were around
twenty church members, ten to fifteen friends, co-workers, and
members from my former church, and the rest was family. After all of
the expected guests had arrived, the doors of the church were locked
just in case of uninvited intruders. There had been rumors of
unhappy church members crashing our wedding, so we weren't
taking any chances.

At 1:05 PM, I was escorted down the aisle. Everything was
charming: the music, the flowers, the decorations, the candles, and

most of all the participants. I wore a lovely two piece champagne, satin, full length suit with rhinestones and matching shoes. Of course, I was nervous, so I focused on remembering my wedding vows to Bobby and my dedication to his kids. I held the vows tightly in my hand and handed them off to my friend Evelyn before walking down the aisle.

Wedding Vows

I had spent a lot of time researching vows appropriate for second marriages involving children. We wanted to include the traditional vows used in the Baptist church, but we also wrote vows to each other and dedications to each other's children.

Vows to Each Other

Mine:
I, Janice, take you, Bobby to be my husband. With the greatest joy, I come into my new life with you. Besides the gift of salvation, you are the most precious gift God has given me. I know that along with the new joys, I face new responsibilities which I cannot fulfill in my own strength. But I can do all things through Christ who strengthens me. By God's grace and power working within me, I desire to be trustworthy as your wife, to serve and love you in all circumstances, to obey you, to allow God to use you to build His qualities in me, as long as God give us life. Bobby, I praise God continually for you and your love and friendship.

Bobby's:
Janice, as we stand before both God and man making public our commitment to one another, I wish to make it known that I recognize God's authority over my life, which is exercised from His loving heart. He has chosen me to be one of His own and has since been my life. I recognize also He has blessed me and entrusted to me your life

as an unearned gift. In recognition of these things, I, Bobby, take you, Janice, to be my wife. I purpose to love you with His love, to provide for your needs through His enablement, and to lead you as He leads me, as long as He gives me life, regardless of circumstances. I promise to allow God to use you in my life as He sees best in building me into His person. I thank Him for your love and friendship.

Dedication to Each Other's Children

Mine:
I want you to know how much I love your father. We have grown closer and desire to spend our lives together. Thank you for sharing your father with me. I promise to be fair and to be honest, to be available for you as I am for your dad, and in due time, to earn your love, respect and true friendship. I will not attempt to replace your mother, but to make a place in your hearts for me. I will be a stepmother and friend, and I will cherish my life with you. On this day when I marry your dad, I promise to love and support you.

Bobby's:
I want you to know I dearly love your mother. Together, we will learn much more about each other. I promise also to be fair and to be honest, to be available for you as I am for your mom, and in due time, to earn your love, respect and true friendship. I will not attempt to replace anyone, but to make a place in your hearts that is for me alone. I will be a stepfather and a friend, and I will cherish my life with both of you.

I Now Pronounce You a Stepfamily

I am not the crying type, but when it came time to say my vows to Bobby, I had to talk slower to keep from crying. My girlfriends said in doing so, I made them cry. When it came time to do the vows to the children, Bobby did his with simplicity. When I requested Bobby's children to come forth, I was reminded by the younger children that their older brothers were sitting in the back of the church. I glanced back and asked them if they would like to participate, but they shook their heads no. Because all eyes were upon us, I wasn't going to allow this awkward moment to disrupt the ceremony, so I continued with the dedication to Jamie and Brandon. We then gave tributes to our parents. My uncle David, who is a minister, gave us a special prayer, our soloist sang a beautiful rendition of the Lord's Prayer, and before we knew it, we were pronounced husband and wife, and Bobby was delighted to salute his bride.

Following the ceremony, we took pictures while the finishing touches were completed for our New Year's dinner on the lower level. My maid of honor quickly came out of her velvet black dress and changed into her apron. The New Year's dinner reception was warm, inviting, and delicious, and everyone had plenty to eat. We left the church around 3:00 PM, went to the house to put a few things together, and headed to the place where we would spend our first night as husband and wife. We came back home the following day to start getting ready for our honeymoon which was five days away.

Keep in mind, as you are busy planning for your marriage to consider all children involved. Family experts Les and Leslie Parrott state it clearly: "Since you are in love and looking toward a future with a new spouse, you may need to take special care to be sure your children feel included and they are part of this major decision that impacts their life" (Parrrott and Parrott 2001, 31). Regardless of whether or not they agree with your decision, it is important to discuss your plans with them and hear and understand their feelings.

Stepmom Survival Tips

1. Seek structured premarital counseling from your pastor or a Christian counselor as soon as you are engaged. Ask if they have experience working with stepfamilies.
2. Talk with the children's biological parents (bio-mom and bio-dad) about getting married and the children's involvement in the ceremony.
3. Discuss your marriage plans with your children even if you plan to elope. Never marry without informing them of your plans.
4. Talk with each child individually to sort out their feelings about the upcoming marriage.
5. Ask for the children's minimal involvement in the wedding, but do not force their participation or attendance.
6. Keep the wedding plans as simple as possible.
7. Include dedications to the children if appropriate.
8. Be prepared for last minute changes or sabotage.
9. Plan to take a honeymoon because you will need it.
10. Enjoy your day and don't let anyone or anything spoil it!

Helpful Scriptures

Proverbs 18:22 (NIV)
He who finds a wife finds what is good and receives favor from the LORD.

Proverbs 25:15 (CEV)
Patience and gentle talk can convince a ruler and overcome any problem.

Proverbs 19:21 (NIV)
Many are the plans in a man's heart, but it is the Lord's purpose that prevails.

Proverbs 13:16 (CEV)
If you have good sense, you will act sensibly, but fools act like fools.

1 John 4:18 (NIV)
There is no fear in love. But perfect love drives out fear, because fear has to do with punishment. The one who fears is not made perfect in love.

Chapter Three
Living-In-Step

Oh, for the days when I was in my prime, when God's intimate friendship blessed my house. Job 29:4 (NIV)

Complicated Circumstances

Once the wedding was over, it was time for a true reality check. There are a few disclaimers as I begin this chapter. In stepfamily literature, there are diverse types of stepfamilies. The variations are based on several factors, including whether or not the biological parents were never married or divorced, where the children reside, and whether or not additional children are added to the union. We were a remarried couple, and both of us had been divorced with children from our previous marriages. By the way, we had no plans whatsoever of having a child together. Eight was enough! I had custody of my children, which meant they would live full time with Bobby and me and visit their father (bio-dad) on alternating weekends. Three of Bobby's children resided with their mother (bio-mom) and would visit our house every other weekend. His oldest three were grown and either in college or living on their own. I learned in my reading that ours was considered one of the more complicated types of stepfamilies because we had children from previous marriages and were noncustodial parents of his children.

Being the pastor and wife didn't help either as we felt like we were living in a glass house, and everyone was watching.

When a newly remarried couple attempts to combine two, fully functioning households who are both rich in tradition and accustomed to their treasured way of life, only one thing can result . . . conflict! The term living-in-step is applied to stepfamilies' everyday way of life. The first rule of thumb for those living-in-step is to comprehend that no one is right or wrong, and conflicts are often the result of differences. A major difficulty for our children was they had to adjust to two sets of household rules; at our home and at their other biological parent's home. In the book *Tying the Family Knot*, author Terri Clark states, "In the biological family, there may be a little rebellion concerning the rules from time to time, but for the most part they are accepted. In the blended family; however, this setup is only half of the child's life. They have another household and another set of rules that may or may not be based on the same values we hold" (Clark 2004, 121).

Following a divorce, kids first of all have to adjust to their parent being a single parent. In the book, *Family Rules,* author Jeannette Lofas shares that as single parents, we are sometimes a little more lenient. Parents' changed behavior is often the result of the guilt of forcing our children to accept changes based on our decisions. I remember the first year following my divorce, when I spent more money and time trying to make up for the perceived damages incurred on my children. After all, I had read literature and family research studies that didn't contain optimistic statistics for children of divorce. One book in particular was *The Unexpected Legacy of Divorce*. Please take the time to read it so you can learn about the effects of divorce on children and parents. After reading the data on children of divorce, I was determined to provide happiness and structure for my children in the midst of their lifestyle changes.

Once remarriage has occurred, the presence of the new spouse significantly changes the circumstances and the environment again. For us, this included additional children who visit only on weekends, along with modifications to household rules. In our new family, the atmosphere was very different on visitation weekends because of so many people in the house. I once read about a blended family that resulted when a vegetarian and a meat eater united. This family compromised by purchasing two refrigerators. Potential problems were alleviated by having the two refrigerators and cooking separate meals, but this solution didn't mean they couldn't sit down and eat at the same time and at the same table. It is important that each member respect the others' choices. Some compromises are easier than others, but even mild changes can be perceived as difficult, especially when children feel like their parent has changed. As you read this chapter, remember I am speaking in first person and sharing my perspective of our experiences. The good news is we enjoyed the same foods, at least for the most part.

My House

Following my divorce, my children and I relocated from Shawnee, Kansas to Olathe, Kansas, which was five to six miles away. It was my custom to do an extensive amount of research on area demographics to determine the areas with the best schools, affordable home prices, and good proximity to work and church. My list of "must haves" included three bedrooms, quick access to the highway, and a garage because I couldn't bear the thought of having to scrape frosted windshields on cold winter mornings. After doing my homework and meeting people at the church, I decided to rent a three bedroom townhouse in a multi-family residential neighborhood. The kids and I moved in and made it our home for six months to see if we wanted to make that community our permanent home. The townhouse was great because there were lots of children around, and it was in a safe neighborhood with great schools. We liked the area so much that within a month of living there I began to look for homes for sale in the area.

As the 2000 New Year began following Y2K, my search for a home intensified and was narrowed to a three mile range in Olathe. I found a realtor and gave her very specific instructions about what we were looking for in a home. My needs included at least a three bedroom house with two living areas, a dining room, a two car garage, and most definitely a fireplace. While I was in the home-buying market, it happened to be a seller's market, so it was very competitive for prospective home buyers. Homes weren't staying on the market very long, and sellers were reviewing several bids and definitely getting their asking price or above. After being outbid on two different homes, I was determined to receive notice whenever a house with my specifications went on the market. My realtor knew I was serious, so she became more aggressive and began notifying me and scheduling viewings the same day a new listing became public. Every available Saturday was spent looking for the perfect house.

One morning in April, my realtor called about a well preserved four bedroom, popular side-to-side split plan, newly listed in the area, and at the right price. I left work early for the showing and immediately fell in love with the neighborhood and the house. She wrote up the offer the same day, and the owners accepted my offer the following day. The sellers had raised their children in the house and had recently retired. They were building their retirement home and would not be able to move until their new home was ready, which would be sometime between June and August. The timeline was perfect because it gave me additional time to save more money. My goal was to occupy the property before school started around the second week in August.

The closing occurred the last week of July, during one of the hottest weeks of the summer. I rented the biggest U-Haul truck I could drive and recruited guys from church, my son, a nephew who was staying with us for the summer, and even my ex-husband to help us move. We had just enough furniture to fill all of the rooms, and there was still plenty of room to spare. Aiden was happy because her room was bigger than the one she had in the townhouse and it was right across from mine, in case she needed to make a mad dash during a late night thunderstorm. Aaron's room was spacious and located on a floor by itself. He was a teenager and appreciated space and privacy. The elementary, junior high, and high school were all within walking distance, and there was an abundance of kids in the neighborhood. After moving in, I promised myself and the kids we would not move again for at least five years. I was adamant about not wanting them to change schools again and planned to stay put until Aaron graduated from high school. I was in year three of my plan when Bobby and I married.

His House

The house Bobby had owned with his former wife had been on the market for over a year and had not yet sold; therefore, he was still the owner of an empty five bedroom, tri-level, single attached home, which now was also legally my property. When they had separated, Bobby moved into his parents' basement apartment that was right around the corner from their old home. Moving in with his parents was a win-win situation for all involved. Bobby's parents were almost eighty years old, and Bobby was a huge help to them. He was able to assist them financially, help out around the house, and be good company for them. Bobby was particularly close to his parents, and they enjoyed having him around.

When Bobby moved from his home originally, he took along limited items, including his home office furniture, personal items, such as clothing, and his book collection. Other than a desk, credenza, and three chairs, he had no other furniture. Fortunately, his parents' basement apartment was fully furnished. The ex-wife moved the rest of the belongings to her apartment about three miles away on the east side of our small town. When they moved, the kids continued to go to the schools in their old neighborhood, so after school they walked to their grandparents' home where Bobby resided. This arrangement was convenient for everyone.

Making Our Home Together

Every stepfamily book I have read suggests newly formed stepfamilies begin their new life together in a new, neutral residence. One of the many advantages of this option includes the fact that many obstacles and problems can be avoided by being proactive and spending time, energy, and money finding a place that works for everyone. With a new place, no one feels invaded, and no one feels unwanted. There are a few extenuating circumstances where it is advised against moving, like during a child's senior year in high school.

As mentioned before, I was still in my five year plan and didn't want to force my children to change schools again. A move of even less than one mile would change the schools my children attended. Moving into Bobby's vacated house was definitely not an option worth considering, so he knew not to even bring it up. He and his former wife had built that home and were very emotionally attached to it. Visitation for his children would have been strange, visiting the house that they used to live in and having other children living in what used to be their space. Because my house had four bedrooms, it would be easier if Bobby moved in with me. Besides, the real estate market had since changed, and it was no longer a seller's market. Houses were a little more difficult to move as indicated by the fact Bobby's house had not sold.

A couple of weeks before the wedding, we began to make plans in preparation for Bobby to move in. There were five children to accommodate every other weekend and only four bedrooms, so room sharing was our only choice. The basement wasn't finished, so we pursued the possibility of adding a bedroom in the basement. The estimate was somewhere in the range of $5,000, which we did not want to invest at the time since we were pondering a future move. We would try to make the best of what we had. Besides, it was only every other weekend, and my son Aaron would only be with us another year. Because Aaron was the oldest, we concluded he would continue to have his own room. Bobby's boys were accustomed to rooming together, so my former office became their bedroom. Our two girls were a year apart in age, so we moved an extra twin bed into Aiden's room to accommodate Jamie. I spoke with Aiden about sharing a room and she was okay with it.

To prepare for our first weekend together, we purchased additional beds, dressers, room decorations, and anything we could think of to help make the transition easier and to make Bobby's kids feel at home during their visits. A drawer was cleaned out in Aiden's dresser for Jamie to store her things. The final touches were made and we felt we were prepared for our first big weekend together as one big happy family. We were not anticipating any problems because Jamie and Brayden had spent the night at my home before and enjoyed staying at my house.

It's Very Dark in Here

At one point in my life, I had suffered from a mild form of narcolepsy, and as a result I had worked hard to perfect the art of sleeping. My requirements included having the darkest, quietist, coolest, bedroom conditions possible. If I couldn't get the room dark enough, I wore what Bobby called "diva blinders" over my eyes. All the bedrooms in or home had ceiling fans and room darkening window coverings. My children appreciated the way my bedroom was set up for sleep and asked that their rooms be prepared the same way; therefore, they were also accustomed to sleeping in dark, quiet, cool bedrooms.

Bobby's kids, on the other hand, were accustomed to having lights on in order to sleep. It was safe to say that they were somewhat afraid of the dark. It was not unusual for them to have a night light or a television on throughout the night. They were also cold natured and mentioned the house being too cold. The lowered temperature had also been one of Bobby's complaints when he came over to visit. The heating thermostat was programmed to lower the temperature even further after 10:00 PM, and then raise it around 6:00 in the morning. Keep in mind we married in January during a cold Kansas winter.

Our first night with all of the kids was a Friday, so we just let the kids do what they wanted to do. They finally went to bed once they had worn themselves out. I didn't worry about noise or televisions because I wanted everybody to be happy. Saturday night was a different story because we had to be at church by 8:00 AM for a First Sunday meeting. Around 10:30 Saturday night, we made sure everyone went to his or her bedrooms to settle down, with the exception of Aaron. Bobby and I finished packing for our honeymoon trip, for we were scheduled to leave following church. All of the lights and televisions were turned off and the house was completely quiet with the exception of Bobby and me discussing what to expect on Sunday. We finally made it to bed around 2:00 in the morning. Not long after we were in bed, there was a knock at the door. Bobby opened the door and Brandon announced, "It's very, very dark in here." When Bobby went to put him back to bed, he discovered Brayden was awake also. He turned on a lamp and a radio, and they were finally able to go to sleep.

We had a larger television in the den and there were televisions in all of the bedrooms for a total of five. I wasn't much of a television watcher and could be in the house alone for hours and never turn one on. My children were limited on the amount of time they could watch television, especially during the week. I had rules about when televisions could be on and demanded all televisions be turned off before going to bed, and televisions were to be turned off if no one was watching them. On Sunday mornings, I preferred to listen to the gospel station instead of watching television. I had read somewhere that sleeping with the television on hindered brain development in children and interrupted productive sleep, so I did not allow my children to stay up into the wee hours of the night watching television even on weekends, or sleep with the television on.

Bobby, on the other hand, had very few restrictions rules related to watching TV. He was used to restricting what they watched, but he didn't impose limitations around when televisions could be on and watched. My rules were difficult for Bobby to enforce with his children because he enjoyed television and had been guilty himself of sleeping all night with the television on before we married. He too was making the adjustment because I needed the television off in order to go to sleep.

In sharing a room, Jamie was used to having the television on when she went to sleep and Aiden was not. Therefore Jamie would often turn the television on after Aiden had fallen asleep. Once the television came on, Aiden woke up and couldn't go back to sleep. After learning that Jamie was turning on the television after she thought Aiden was asleep, I learned to go in later and turn it off. Brayden and Brandon also found it difficult to sleep without the television on and would often turn it back on when we went to bed.

Whenever Bobby's children slept over on school nights, I refused to lighten up on my "no sleeping with the TV on" rule. Soon Bobby learned to compromise by setting the off timer for thirty minutes to an hour. Although the television was in another room, our bedroom was right across the hall, and the noise or light managed to disturb my sleep, even with the doors closed. Of course, the boys would turn it back on because they were afraid of the dark. Therefore, I often got up in the middle of the night or first thing in the morning to turn the TV off.

It frustrated me that they would turn the television back on after I had instructed them to turn it off. Turning the television back on was a serious issue for me because I needed all the sleep I could get. I don't know which was more frustrating for me, not getting sleep or knowing they had deliberately defied my rules. One weekend, I was so irritated they had disobeyed my television policy, I conveniently displaced the remote control so they could not turn the TV back on and further disturb my sleep. The rest of the night I felt bad about it and guilty because just as I needed silence in order to sleep, they needed the background noise that the television provided.

House Rules

Before my last name became Love, I had very limited house rules for the three of us. I encouraged the kids to be in bed by a certain time, to clean up when I asked them to, and to give me peace and quiet when I needed it. Aaron and Aiden knew their chores and when they needed to be done. My kids never argued about what to watch on television because they had their own televisions. They never fought over the telephone or computer time. There wasn't much left to question, because everyone knew what they were supposed to do. After marrying, I didn't want to impose any new rules on my children because they would most likely blame the changes on Bobby's presence.

Because Bobby was living at his parents' house, he really hadn't established many rules for when his kids came to visit him on weekends. Often single men do not establish a whole lot of rules because they want their children to be happy while they are visiting. Most of the time, they were not home or the kids were outside playing. After a few weekends, it didn't take long to figure out that our children were accustomed to being in two vastly different environments. I was used to functioning as a custodial parent, and Bobby was used to being an every other weekend parent.

The more people there are in a house, the greater the opportunity for confusion, which we began to experience after a month of being married. As a result, we had to think about how we would develop rules for our household. How were chores to be divided, what about curfews, telephone rules, computer time? Most of all, how would we communicate these rules to everyone and make sure everything was fair and equitable? I was in a delicate situation because I wanted to keep my own kid's lives as normal as possible, yet at the same time, I didn't want to appear bossy and demanding to Bobby's kids because I didn't want them to think I was mean.

Noise Level

One of the first things Bobby noticed and mentioned when he moved into our home was how it stayed quiet most of the time. With my children being seven years apart, they rarely played together and often spent time alone in their rooms. As Aaron grew older, he played his stereo in his bedroom, but his room was on a different level so we couldn't hear any noise. Even though Aiden's room was right across from ours, she watched television or played her game-boy and played quietly. On average, the phone rang once or twice in an evening, and the caller was typically a telemarketer. Aaron and Aiden rarely talked on the phone, and I usually answered the phone whenever it rang. There were three phones in the house, and none of them were located in the children's bedrooms. We had call waiting, but it was rarely used. Overall, we had a pretty quiet house, and I liked it that way. I had a term that I used with my children called "QT" which meant, quiet time. Whenever I said, "QT," my kids knew to shut it down. Our quiet time was practiced regularly after I tucked Aiden in the bed which was around 9:15 on weeknights. On weekends, I rarely requested for the house to be quiet.

Bobby and his children were accustomed to a higher noise level at home. With so many children in the house, there was always someone around, and they had frequent visitors. Conversations were continuous, the telephone rang often, and all of the televisions in the house were on regardless of whether or not someone was watching them. Bobby's kids were very social and had lots of friends. They were allowed and encouraged to answer the phone, and to be respectful and answer call waiting calls if they were on the phone when another call came in.

During our visitation weekends, the phone began ringing on Friday afternoons after school and continued to ring until late Friday night, as well as on Saturday and Sunday. Bobby and I were the only ones who had cell phones, so the kids' calls came to our home phone. I wasn't used to hearing the phone ringing constantly, being interrupted by call waiting, and kids answering the telephone. Hearing kids yelling across the house at one another to pick up the phone was an irritant for me. To keep my sanity, I imposed a thirty minute limit on phone calls and timed them. If the limit was exceeded, I picked up the phone to announce the call had been long enough. After a month or two of the phone ringing off the hook, I stopped answering the phone and wanted to unplug them all and throw them out the window.

Our house was a side-to-side split, which meant there were four sets of stairs. There were stairs to the basement where the laundry area was, stairs from the main level to the family room, stairs from the main level to the bedroom level, and another set to Aaron's bedroom. Again, before Bobby and his kids, there was very little movement between levels. When I was growing up, my mom had an issue with slamming the screen door; now my issue was running up and down the stairs. I had always demanded that children walk up and down the stairs because we had lived in houses with steep stairways. Bobby's kids, especially the boys, were athletic and accustomed to jogging the stairs, which made the same amount of noise as running in my opinion. Just another minor thing that drove me nuts because there was always a reason to come up or down the stairs to find out where the action was or to see who was on the caller ID.

Bedtimes

Bedtimes in my home had already been established and observed faithfully. Aaron was allowed to stay up later, as long as he had his bath out of the way before 10:30 p.m. I did not want him to start his bath too late because the pipes made a loud noise when the shower was turned on, and the noise would startle me as I was trying to fall asleep. Aiden had to be in the bed by 9:00 on weeknights. Whenever Bobby's kids were over during the week particularly school nights, we informed every one of their bedtime and reminded them that the television and lights needed to be off.

I usually worked at full steam throughout the week and then collapsed on Friday nights. I often walked in the house, kicked off my shoes, and fell asleep on the couch, waiting on everyone to decide what to eat for dinner. There were few appointments on our schedule for Saturday mornings, intentionally so. On Friday nights, the kids stayed awake until midnight or one, watching television, talking, or playing. When they reached the point that they could barely stay awake, they gave up and went to bed on their own.

Saturday nights were a different story. With Bobby being a pastor, he often needed quiet time on Saturday evenings to put the finishing touches on his sermons. I also used the time to review and prepare for my Sunday school class. Staying up late on Saturday nights was not a problem until I noticed Bobby's children stretched out in the pews or their heads bobbing during church service. Oh Lord no! I was not going to allow any children of mine over the age of five to sleep during church. We had to make some adjustments in Saturday bedtimes, not only to keep kids awake during church, but so that everyone could get up early enough for us to make it to Sunday school on time.

Cleanliness is Next to Godliness

There were a total of two and a half bathrooms in our home. One full bath was part of the master bedroom, and the other was shared by our children on the bedroom level. The half bathroom was located next to the family room on the lower level. At night, hot water was a premium with five showers to be taken, so we scheduled them strategically. The shower order went from the youngest to the oldest. The schedule began with Brandon, and everyone was encouraged to clean up behind themselves. Aiden didn't like getting out of the tub and finding a wet rug, so she negotiated with Brandon to take her bath first. Bathing would begin around 8:00 PM with twenty minutes in between, and the last one being complete by 10:30.

We installed extra racks in the bathroom so everyone had a place to hang their wet towels, but it seemed as though towels were growing out of the walls. Not wanting to make the kids responsible for washing the towels, I started washing the massive pile of towels on Sunday evenings after the Love children left. After a full weekend with all of the kids, I required my kids to clean their bathroom on Monday or Tuesday. They didn't think it was fair for them to clean up after everyone else, but I demanded that they do it. They cleaned the bathroom, but complained that they didn't make the mess by themselves. After listening to their complaints for a few months, we finally assigned the bathroom cleaning to the youngest two during visitation weekend. This worked out well because they appeared to enjoy having a chore to call their own. Looking back, it would have been helpful if we had an additional bathroom, one for the boys and one for the girls, because five children using one bathroom was difficult to manage, especially in the morning.

As visitation weekend approached, Bobby began a cleaning frenzy to prepare the rooms for the kids. The boys' room doubled as the ironing room and the closet contained my wardrobe overflow. As I decided what to wear to work on weekdays, it was not uncommon to find three suits and several boxes of shoes on the bed. Thursday evening was when I would typically clean it up. Sometimes Bobby beat me to it when he knew I had a busy schedule, or he thought the kids would be over before I got around to it.

Because Aiden and Jamie shared a room, Bobby would also go into Aiden's room and make adjustments as needed to make preparations for Jamie. I sometimes felt guilty about Bobby cleaning up Aiden's room when it was her job to do so, but in my opinion the room was fine. It would have been uncomfortable for Bobby to ask Aiden to straighten things because Jamie was coming over. Rather than saying anything to Aiden or Bobby, I continued to let Bobby do whatever he needed to do in preparation for our weekend with his children.

As chores are being assigned, it is important to be sensitive to the children, however you may end up hearing "it's not fair" frequently. If the children who reside in the home have to clean up behind the ones that visit, they will complain the other ones never have to do any work. They may even accuse them of being spoiled and lazy. On the other hand, if the visiting children have chores to do at their regular place of residence, they may feel like it is not fair to have to do chores at both houses and comment that the mess was there before they ever got there. To keep peace and at the same time not over work yourself, make a list of chores and be fair in assigning them and discuss them with the children as soon as possible.

Bigger Doesn't Always Mean Better

Around year three, we casually began to look for a house to purchase in both of our names. We needed to remain in the Olathe area because of our church and the desire to remain in the same school district. I wanted to get a little closer to work, for I was driving roughly thirty seven miles each way to the Missouri side. Because Bobby's parents were elderly, it was important to him that they are able to drive to our house with relative ease. We also wanted to be close to his children, but not so close that our kids would be in the same schools. We only had to accommodate four children, because my son Aaron was attending college in North Carolina. Our decision to move was put on the fast track when Bobby decided to run for office in a district on the east side of town. The east and west sides are separated by Interstate 35, and there were only two main streets at the time that crossed over the highway.

After looking at the district political boundaries, we narrowed the vicinity to a four square mile region. Of course, we wanted a mansion on a limited budget. We wrote our wants and needs in a notebook and titled it "Our Yellow House" which included a list of features we wanted for our dream home. We needed at least four bedrooms (five would have been perfect), living space galore, a finished basement, a sizeable, inviting kitchen, substantial bedroom space, including a master bedroom with a sitting area, a large walk in closet for all of my shoes, and as many bathrooms as possible. In our spare time, we used the services of a realtor from our church and began our search for the perfect house for our blended family weekends. We decided on a four bedroom home that met most of our criteria. A few drawbacks included white carpet and not having additional bathrooms or the Hollywood style, where two bedrooms connect with their own sink and vanity, but have a shared tub/shower and commode in the middle. In spite of the white carpet and a bathroom shortage, we pretty much had the other desires listed in "Our Yellow House" notebook.

Although we had not sold the house we were living in, we purchased the home we believed would work for us. We finally moved into our new home during Memorial Day weekend. Packing was difficult because we were trying to keep the house clean for possible showings. Seven days later, we had moved everything out of the old house and placed it haphazardly in the new one. I was used to having somewhat of an organized move, and this one was anything but. We had assistance from a few friends and family members to move the big things, but in packing and moving the smaller boxes, we were on our own.

Our new house was substantially larger than the home we moved from, which was going to create a noticeable inequity in the living arrangements for Bobby's children. We were worried that our new home would create more tension between us and them, and as a result, we would end up back in court paying a child support increase. New car purchases had created conflict in the past, so we knew a larger house would definitely signal trouble. Because of our concerns, we did not ask Bobby's children to assist us in our move. We were in the house for two weeks before they came over for a visit. Looking back, we should have included his children in our search and the move so that they would have felt included in our accomplishment. Of course hindsight is 20/20.

In this house, the girls had their own bedrooms but the boys still had to share. Having the boys share a bedroom was the best solution since Brayden only had a few years left before leaving for college. We were trying to figure out how to set up a bedroom in the basement for Brayden, but decided to turn it into my office because of the built in desks. The only place for the bed would have been against a door which would have seemed awkward and frightening. We purchased a double bed for Jamie's room and decorated it nicely. The boys' room was arranged similarly to the way it was at the former house. Aiden got the queen bed that used to be in Aaron's room at the former house.

I worked tirelessly to prepare the rooms for the kids' first weekend at our new house. I even bought an air hockey table and placed it in the basement for recreation. We were fortunate to have a built in basketball goal for the boys. The kids seemed to love the house, but we didn't have enough televisions and cable hookups to give every bedroom television access. This left Jamie temporarily without a television in her room. Whenever my son Aaron came home from North Carolina for the holidays or for a summer break, he didn't seem to mind making his home in the basement. There was a full bathroom and the couch was a sleeper sofa. It soon became known as the bachelor pad, and Bobby's son Brayden claimed it as his own space once Aaron returned to North Carolina.

Learning from Mistakes

Looking back, we may have fared better if Bobby and I had bought another house as soon as we married. We stayed in my house for three years. Bobby and I discussed our living arrangements often, and Bobby had shared repeatedly feeling uncomfortable moving to an established home. From a man's point of view, it was difficult for Bobby to just walk in because he didn't feel like he was bringing anything to the table. Having been the family provider for most of his adult life, he found it challenging to walk into a situation where the female provided the home, furniture, and the major necessities. When Bobby first arrived, I supported him in rearranging whatever he wanted to and encouraged him as the head of the household. I happily turned the garage over to him to do as he pleased. At one stage, we turned the formal living room into his office to give him exclusive space.

Always keep in mind household patterns, schedules, and rules are already established and ingrained and most often difficult to change. According to Bobby, the newcomer has to find his or her way, learn the nuances, protocols, and boundaries. He reminded me often that at times he felt like he and his offspring were aliens invading our space. He admitted placing a tremendous amount of pressure on himself because he didn't want to come in and upset the apple cart. On Friday evenings when he picked up his kids, he tested the waters to see what type of moods his kids were in and tried to let them download as much as possible before they arrived at our house. Out of nervousness, he often huddled his children to explain protocols, what to do, what not to do, and gave pre-visit instructions that included don't be loud, be cordial, speak, don't make a mess, clean up what you mess up, and anything else he thought might bother me.

The other area Bobby struggled in was his children feeling like they couldn't claim anything as their own. When we went out and bought dressers and provided space to store their belongings, we believed that they would leave a few belongings behind. The drawers in Aiden's room prepared for Jamie were rarely used. We hung up posters on the walls also to make them feel at home, but Bobby never felt like we did enough. He encouraged his kids to bring things from home, but they rarely did. A couple of times, they brought their gaming system. Usually everyone played with Aaron and Aiden's things, which fortunately wasn't a problem. Because Bobby seemed so unsettled about the matter, I tried to explain to him that my daughter considered her room at her dad's house like a motel room. Everything she took with her always came back. She may have left pajamas and toothbrushes there, but everything else was brought back home.

I never felt like I was successful in helping Bobby's kids to see our home as their home. Just visiting on weekends or occasionally made it difficult to feel like home. For a new stepfamily, I think it is important to give everyone his or her space as much as possible and try to make everyone comfortable. I cannot overstate the importance of realizing that a new normal has to be established and to combine former household rules into new ones that apply to the newly established household. New rules can be explained by using the following phrase. "In this house, we _____." For example, "In this house we turn off lights when we leave the room." Flexibility is important as well as some give and take. Most importantly relax, don't let little things turn into major frustrations for you, and do not let your home become uncomfortable for you and your spouse.

Stepmom Survival Tips

1. Before marriage, plan to locate or purchase a new home together.
2. If remaining in the same location, make necessary changes to help everyone feel welcomed.
3. As finances allow, move into a home that meets everyone's needs as much as possible.
4. Involve everyone in finding a new home and decorating decisions.
5. Try to give everyone private space.
6. Establish new family rules together.
7. Plan a family meeting to discuss household rules.
8. Keep the lines of communication open.
9. Establish and agree on rules around television, computer and internet use, and telephones.
10. Decide and discuss how chores will be done particularly related to the kitchen and bathrooms.

Helpful Scriptures

Psalm 127:1 (NIV)
Unless the LORD builds the house, its builders labor in vain. Unless the LORD watches over the city, the watchmen stand guard in vain.

Psalm 137:4 (NIV)
How can we sing the songs of the LORD while in a foreign land?

Proverbs 24:3-4 (NIV)
By wisdom a house is built, and through understanding it is established; through knowledge its rooms are filled with rare and beautiful treasures.

Leviticus 27:14 (NIV)
If a man dedicates his house as something holy to the LORD, the priest will judge its quality as good or bad. Whatever value the priest then sets, so it will remain.

Proverbs 14:1 (CEV)
A woman's family is held together by her wisdom, but it can be destroyed by her foolishness.

Chapter Four
What's My Name?

A good name is more desirable than great riches; to be esteemed is better than silver or gold. Proverbs 22:1 (NIV)

The Name Game

In a traditional biological home, the lady of the house is referred to as Mom or Mother or a variation of either. The male of the household is referred to as Father or Dad. It was no different for our children. Bobby's kids called him Dad, and my children called me Mom. When divorce occurs, there are no ex-parents, only ex-spouses. Children do not stop calling their parents mom and dad just because they are divorced. When remarriage occurs, calling the stepparent by the name that has been reserved for the biological parent can create loyalty issues for the children.

Names are important to people. Someone once said that a person's name is important to them and the sweetest sound to their ears. Starbucks gains customer loyalty by calling their client's name when their beverage is ready. As mentioned in my introduction, for the purposes of this book, all of our children have been given fictitious names they chose themselves. As they were selecting their alternative names, they wanted trendy names to represent them. We spent time on name websites, and they devoted extensive discussion as to what they wanted to be called. Also you may have noticed in your reading,

I am referring to our ex-spouses as bio-parents. My children's father is referred to as bio-dad and the mother of Bobby's children is referred to as bio-mom.

About two weeks before the wedding, Bobby and I had a discussion about what we wanted to be called by our stepchildren. I had observed other families and had done unofficial research by talking with other stepmoms to ascertain what they were being called. In my questioning, I also sought to understand their methodology and reasoning. In many families, the stepparent was simply called by their first name. Although they were usually comfortable with this and may have even suggested to be called by their first names, I found this appalling. Based on what I was taught as a child, you could almost never call adults by their first name. Even as an adult, there are still people from my childhood I would not dare call by their first name, even to this day.

In our Baptist church setting, most people refer to one another as brother or sister, followed by their last name. Prior to marrying Bobby, I was referred to by most church members as Sister Turner. The children of my lifetime closest friends who were not part of our church usually referred to me as Miss Janice. Because Bobby was a pastor, most people referred to him as Pastor Love or Reverend Love. There were some church workers who were comfortable with being called by their first name, but I was not one of them. Even when one of the youth workers had requested that our children call her by her first name, I instructed my children to call her by her formal name or put "Miss" in front of her first name.

As we had discussions around what to be called, we both decided the first name basis would not work for us. We wanted our children to live by the same rules by which we were raised, which meant children should be respectful and never call an adult by their first name. We spent a great deal of time talking about this between the two of us, but we never had the conversation with the children prior to the wedding. With our short window before January arrived, we had plenty of other things to worry about. Before we knew it, we were married, and it was too late to have those critical conversations. We decided respect was more important than the name itself.

Accidental Name Calling

After returning from our honeymoon, we had a small reception. Following the reception, as we were loading up our cars to go home, something interesting happened. All of us could not ride in one car, so we asked one of Bobby's children to ride with my friend Tina. When asked where he was going, he stated, "To Sister Turner's house." Tina giggled because she knew the way he answered and said, "Sister Turner," he perhaps didn't realize my name had changed. Everyone else was silent including me because it wasn't a teachable moment to inform my new stepson, I now had the same last name he had with a new driver's license to prove it.

Not knowing what to call me, Bobby's kids continued to call me Sister Turner, said "uh," or just started talking. I knew they were struggling, so I made it easy on them by responding when I knew they were talking to me. Our third weekend together, Bobby's two youngest children Jamie and Brandon asked Bobby if they could call me Mom. Bobby said it was fine as long as they were okay with it. As a result the younger two called me mom for the next several weekends. Brayden continued to call me Sister Turner. Finally, one day I couldn't take it any longer and reminded him very gently that I now had a new last name. Making mention of what my name was turned out to be a mistake, and for quite a while it was pure avoidance and no conversation from him.

Several months after we were married, during a visitation weekend, we noticed that Jamie and Brandon began calling me by my first name. I didn't think I had heard it right, so didn't pay much attention at first. After it happened several times, I was bewildered. At an opportune moment I asked what had changed and why I was not being called Mom anymore. The response blew me away. I was informed that an older sibling had told them to stop calling me Mom because it made their mother upset. I was left speechless, not knowing what to say. Bobby and I discussed how we should handle knowing about the brother's influence, and he didn't know what to say or do either. We left it alone for a while until I began to notice that there was not only a name change, but also an attitude change.

We observed that my kids were still calling Bobby by his official title, Reverend Love, even at home. This wasn't perfect, but at least Bobby felt respected. However, Bobby had a similar first name incident happen to him when he accompanied Aaron to pick up his driver's permit. Bobby's version went like this: "While we were standing in the lobby, in front of God and all humanity, Aaron called me Bobby." When they returned home, Bobby was offended, and I totally understood his frustration. Regarding the name game, Bobby and I felt like we were going down a road in which there was no return, and we didn't know how to fix it.

No Name at All

In my opinion, there is only one thing worse than being called by a name that you don't like: it's not being acknowledged at all. During the first three years of our marriage, we had to attend events where our children were being honored. These occasions were usually sponsored by the schools or other organizations our children were involved in. If the child's name was announced, it was customary to say that they were the son or daughter of whomever. What would often happen was the child was asked who their parents were. Naturally, they named their biological parents and didn't mention the stepparents. For Bobby's children, the announcement typically ended up being read as the son or daughter of Rev. Bobby Love and Mrs. (bio-mom) Love. The way the names were listed, it sounded as though they were still married. It appeared even worse in print. Early in our marriage, I was never even acknowledged. At most events of this nature, we were on pins and needles waiting to see what was going to be said or written. As expected, we were often disappointed.

Even when we tried to be proactive and ask in advance, nothing changed. We were thankful there were no weddings coming up any time soon. It did improve once the bio-mom remarried because now she had a different last name and two stepparents had to be included.

Early in our marriage, Bobby's daughter Jayden was elected as the president of the state youth convention for our church affiliation. Being in this position was a big deal for her, our church, and our family, and we were very proud. It is customary at the youth convention for the president to give an annual address. The programs were printed in advance which included a picture and bio of Jayden. When we arrived at the annual president's night, we noticed that her bio did not include any mention of me, nor was I even acknowledged during the program. It was really awkward because we were sitting on the stage with Jayden. Both Bobby and I were hurt and wanted to lash out at the adults who knew better. The good news is, the second time around, (she was president for two years) both our names were listed and a general statement of acknowledgement given. "I want to thank all my parents for being here." No personal recognition, but at least it was a start.

As always, I sought help from any written resources I could find. One book suggested having family meetings to discuss names and titles. Based on the recommendation, we called a family meeting with all of the children in the household. Bobby led the discussion by stating adults in our household would not be called by our first names. I remained silent even though my children were part of the conversation. He then added, "Whatever we were going to be called needed to be a version of Mom or Dad or Miss Janice, or for him Reverend Love." Our children heard him literally, and the results of the meeting were my children calling Bobby, Reverend Love and his children calling me Miss Janice. Not quite the results we were expecting.

In the book *Parenting the Other Chick's Eggs,* Ruth-Ann Clurman wrote, "A word is only as ugly or bothersome as the intent of the person saying it. If any name is said with pride, honor is attached to the word." She, as well as other resources suggested the use of terminology that is least confusing to children. The more we thought about it, we knew that we had messed up by the way we conducted our meeting. Most importantly, we did not allow our children to have input or make recommendations on what was most comfortable for them. Having everyone together was not the best suggestion either. It may have helped for us to talk with our own children. We needed another plan.

I was not happy with Bobby being called reverend anything by my children, because it seemed so formal. A teachable moment presented itself, and I discussed with Aiden about what Bobby may want to be called that acknowledged him as a father figure. I reassured her he was not trying to take her dad's place, but that he was a father figure in our home and needed to be respected as such. I left her with a few suggestions when she could not come up with something on her own. Within a few days she had come to a decision. One day she asked Bobby for something and referred to him as S-Dad, which is short for stepdad. To Bobby it sounded more like Super-Dad, so he was quite happy with her choice. From that point on, he affectionately became known to Aiden as S-Dad. Aaron didn't catch on at first, but eventually began to also refer to him as S-Dad. Bobby was comfortable with what my children called him. Luckily for him, I was very deliberate in my conversations with my children that he was the adult father figure in our home and needed to be respected as such, even if he wasn't their father.

On the other hand, I was called Janice a few more times, particularly by the older children and occasionally the younger children. I finally concluded that the bio-mom referred to me as Janice when discussing me with her children. Bobby began to see my frustration and addressed it openly whenever it happened in his presence. He even had a few behind the scenes meetings with the kids to try to get them to call me Mom again, but they would not budge. I did not realize that he was having these conversations which in a sense only made the situation worse. I'm sure his children were confused because their mom was saying to call me one thing, and their dad was saying to call me another. As usual, their mom won. As Bobby says, "Mama said."

They Are Not Your Children

I finally realized that the name game was a battle between the bio-mom and me. Late fall, Bobby's kids were staying with us for a week because the bio-mom was entertaining out of town guests. During the week, we had an extreme weather change, and I needed to get the children's coats from the bio-mom's house. I called in advance to mention that we would be stopping by after work to pick up coats and wanted to make sure we did not disturb her. I also mentioned that the kids had come home with a note indicating their lunch accounts needed some attention. I suggested she give the school a call to check on their lunch accounts.

Once the children returned home, the bio-mom and I engaged in an unfriendly conversation regarding my perceived interference. I was told that they were not my children. I retaliated by explaining that because I paid insurance on them, they were officially my children too. Bad move on my part. Now I had launched a competition between myself and the bio-mom and gave her the impression I was trying to take her kids away from her. In return, this fear strongly influenced her behavior and put the kids in the position of loyalty conflict and that they had to make a choice between me and her. Unfortunately, our conversation was shared with the children, who then wanted to ease their mother's concerns as much as possible. The only way to ease her concerns was not to establish an intimate relationship with me.

Trial and Error

I don't give up easily, so I was determined to speak with Bobby's children myself. Things had been tense in the household, so I made it a point to try to spend special one on one time with Bobby's kids. I decided to start with the younger boys. We made an agreement for me to spend private time with them individually during weekend visitation. The outing lasted an hour at the location of the child's choosing. To keep from spending a small fortune and not wanting to appear as though I was buying their love, the cost of the activity could not exceed five dollars per person. The other prerequisite was they had to telephone me no later than Thursday night to let me know the activity they wanted to do. After giving them a few suggestions, they got pretty creative, and we did things like going to the mall, to the video arcade, the library, grocery store or anything else that met the budget restrictions. On one occasion, I even went to laser tag (a stretch for me) and got killed several times, fortunately not by my stepson.

As we enjoyed our outings, we chatted about a variety of topics, such as what was going on in school, sports and team activities, or just general areas of interest to them. As we were out doing fun stuff, I tried to find a way to ease into stepfamily subject matter. Not wanting to make the conversation distressing for them, I asked questions like "What would make you feel more comfortable in our home?" I'm not sure if they felt secure enough to give me an honest answer, because I never received any suggestions.

During one outing, I asked if I could share what was important to me. My needs included: a phone call every now and then; a hug whenever they came over; and thirdly, being called something other than Miss Janice. Brandon and Brayden and I finally agreed that we would have our own little secret, and they would call me MJ, which stood for Mom Janice. However, the rest of the group thought it meant Miss Janice. I hadn't informed Bobby of my conversation with the boys so when he heard them call me MJ, he was offended. He told them not to call me that because it was disrespectful. At this point the kids were once again confused and defaulted back to what was most comfortable for them, Miss Janice. In a conversation with the bio-mom, I soon discovered that the title of mom or anything related was a trophy term which had only been reserved for her; therefore, I had no rights to the title in any form. Both she and the kids felt I had not earned the honors and decided they would call me Miss Janice. Therefore, that was the rule, and they were sticking to it.

"Miss Janice" It Is

As I mentioned earlier, I did have a few friends whose children called me Miss Janice and I didn't have a problem with it. In fact my children addressed their stepmom with a Miss in front of her name, and it worked for them. Even though I have never asked her if she prefers being called something else, I did make suggestions to Aiden to find something else to call her. Aiden assured me it was fine with the bio-dad and her stepmom. They have even signed cards and written ads for my children confirming their choice.

Again, even though it worked for others, I wasn't satisfied with my stepchildren calling me Miss Janice. There's something about being in a mothering role and not being acknowledged fondly. After all, when they were with us, I cooked for them, cleaned up after them, and provided for them. Again, in my mind, "Miss Janice" seemed cold, unloving, and the title continued to emphasize I was not accepted as their stepmother. In public settings, especially at church, I felt even worse when my stepchildren would refer to me as Miss Janice. Not that I wanted everyone to believe that we were the perfect family, but I felt it drew attention to us not functioning very well as a family unit.

Over time I began to resent being called Miss Janice. Each and every time I was addressed by that name, it was just a reminder that often saddened me. When I was in the worst of moods, it almost felt like being called out of my name. I wanted so much to be loved and respected by them, and wanted a good stepmom name. Was my ego getting the best of me? Looking back, I was probably more frustrated that someone who did not live in my home was dictating what I was called. My ego took control, and I began to feel justified that I should be angry about the way I was being treated.

I mentioned it to Bobby on a few occasions, but he said he didn't know what to do. He empathized with me and wanted to make me feel better, so he decided to talk to the kids once again. Bobby and I often took separate vacations with our children. During one of their vacations, he had individual conversations with the three younger ones to talk about life, me, and whatever else needed to be addressed. He seized the opportunity to mention that I did not like being called Miss Janice. He reasoned as to how they would feel if someone lived in their home and took care of them, and the person called them miss or mister. He also spoke about how they called other people by the title of mister or miss and how much more I should mean to them. He also suggested that they each talk to me one on one and find out what I wanted to be called.

About a month later, on the way to church, Jamie asked if she could talk with me when we returned home. During our conversation, we discussed the past and how difficult it had been in the beginning for her having a stepmom. She said she now saw things differently. Something happened at school to cause her to think. In one of her classes, the teacher asked everyone to discuss their parents' professions. Jamie mentioned she could describe what her mother and father did for a living, but all she knew about my employment was I worked at a health center and that I helped people. She felt embarrassed because she did not know more about me. I acknowledged that we had gotten off to a bad start, but I was forgiving and ready to move forward. We agreed that she would call me S-Mom. The title lasted all of about two weekends, and I have not heard it since. The boys were back to calling me MJ and the other ones called me by my least favorite title, Miss Janice.

Whenever Bobby's oldest son Bryson calls, he instinctively calls me Moms. He always refers to Bobby as Pops. I'm not sure why he felt comfortable with calling me Moms. Maybe it's because he is not the biological child of the bio-mom, even though he was raised with the rest of the Love children. Bryson and I never had a discussion, I guess it just happened. On the other hand, after eight to nine years of being called Miss Janice, I had given up hope. As I revealed excerpts from this book to Bobby's daughter Janae, she responded by sharing she was sensitive to my feelings about what she called me and didn't know I felt the way I did. My prayer was answered when she asked if I had a preference being called MJ. As of now, only one child calls me Miss Janice. Five out of six isn't bad!

Grandchildren

A few years into our marriage, a wonderful miracle happened in our lives. Bobby's son Bryson had fathered a child (Mason), but Bobby had not seen his eleven year old grandson for a few years. Unbeknownst to us, Mason and his mother lived within two miles of us. One day, we saw him and his mother briefly exiting an elevator at the local hospital as we were going to do a hospital visit with one of our church members. He did not recognize who Bobby was and surely didn't have a clue who I was. His mother was very cordial and spoke to us, and later when Mason asked, she told him that Bobby was his grandpa. At the same time, Bobby informed me who Mason was. I felt bad that we had a grandson with whom we were not in communion, especially with Mason's father living out of state. Eventually fate intervened, and Mason's mom contacted us with a thought provoking email. After reading the email, I contacted his mother indicating a desire to establish a relationship with them. I had breakfast with her and discussed Bobby and me being a part of Mason's life. We had just missed his 11th birthday, so it was a perfect excuse to send him something in the mail. We were blessed to find them, and it was important to us Mason feel loved and accepted by our family.

I excitedly purchased a birthday card and a gift card and mailed them along with some pictures of us. Bobby and I talked about how to sign the card. The card sat on the counter for two days waiting on us to decide what we wanted to be called by our grandson. I had a running joke with my kids that I was too cool to be called by anything old sounding like Grandma. Aiden poked fun at me and said that she and Aaron's kids were going to call me Granny or Grandma. I proudly repeated regularly that all of my grandchildren were going to call me "Cool Mama J," and to make sure I was going to print it in on my license plate after I turned 65. When it came down to the moment, I signed the birthday card, Mama J.

Two days after I mailed the envelope, I got a phone call from Mason, thanking us for the card. During the call, I asked his mother if we could take him on an outing during the weekend to do something fun. She excused herself for a second and yelled to Mason. She informed him that Mama J wanted to know if he wanted to hang out with us on Saturday. He screamed in the background, "Yes!" Our first outing with him was a blast. We had some furniture shopping to do, so we took him along with us. It may have been boring for most kids, but Mason had a ball trying out all the new furniture and selecting the pieces to complete his dream bedroom.

Mason is a warm hearted kid with lots of energy and a great sense of humor. Hide and seek became our game at the furniture store while in the kids section. He hid and then yelled out, "Mama J, you can't find me." It seemed natural for him to call me Mama J, and he had just met me. I can't help but wonder what my future step-grandchildren will call me and what our lives will be like as grandparents' living-in-step. Maybe that's a future book.

Maybe It's Just Me

You may be saying to yourself, what is the issue here if they never called you out of your name? I guess it was that I wasn't raised that way. As children, we were taught to respect adults and never to call them by their first name. Even today, I respect my elders and address them properly. When I married Bobby, I had no problems addressing his mother as Mom. I still referred to my former mother-in-law as Mom until she passed away a few years ago.

For anyone out there getting ready to get married, if this could possibly be an issue for you, I would strongly suggest that you talk with your future spouse beforehand, and discover what is comfortable for you. My point here is that kids will call you whatever their parents instruct them to call you. I can't stress enough discussing this before the marriage and not leaving it to chance. Talk it over with your partner and then discuss it with the children. Give them examples and choices and offer explanations regarding your wishes.

Be careful that this issue does not become a source of anger and frustration for you. Understand that even though you are a stepmom, you are not a replacement mother, even if the bio-mom is deceased. Don't make this a battle for motherhood rights because you are not their mother. Whatever you are called should reflect your role in your stepchildren's lives. God really had to deal with me, for He helped me to realize that I was brought into my stepchildren's lives to be a support, not a parent. After all, they had a mother who was a very good one. Once I took self out of the way, I guess it really didn't matter to me as long as I feel like they care about me and respect me for who and what I am to them. If you are already in the thick of things and don't like what you are being called, pray for the wisdom to discuss it with your husband and his children. Please don't let thoughts about what your stepchildren call you to fester, and cause you to be angry every time you talk to them. If you have children, set the example by talking with them sincerely about what they should call your husband.

While having a conversation with a co-worker, she mentioned that her siblings were upset with her for not calling her father's wife Mom. I took the time to explain to her the stepmom's side of the story and suggested she find something endearing to call her. She acknowledged it was going to be difficult, but she would at least think about it. About a week later, I was in my office and an e-mail arrived in my inbox. She thanked me for our conversation regarding the subject matter and told me she had found a more endearing term for her stepmother, and that she was going to call her Mom Rose from now on. I got up from my desk and ran down the stairs to find my coworker. I gave her a hug and thanked her for making my day. She couldn't understand why I was so happy. I just saw it as another victory for a stepmom out there who was feeling unloved.

Stepmom Survival Tips

1. The choice of what to call the stepparent should be a deliberate choice.
2. Decide whether or not being called by your first name is comfortable for you.
3. Decide how you want adults to be referred to in your home.
4. Don't just wait and see what happens.
5. Discuss name options as a couple before making recommendations to the children.
6. Be careful not to demand a title that by rights belongs to someone else.
7. Talk openly with the kids before the marriage and provide them with appropriate step parent name options or examples.
8. If you are being called something you are uncomfortable with, address it immediately and resolve the issue.
9. Whatever you are called, remember if it is done with respect and admiration, it doesn't matter.
10. Consider grandchildren and how to explain their new step-grandparent and what to call them. Think about future generations and the legacy you want to leave.

Helpful Scriptures

Proverbs 3:3-5 (NIV)
Let love and faithfulness never leave you; bind them around your neck, write them on the tablet of your heart. Then you will win favor and a good name in the sight of God and man.

Ecclesiastes 7:1 (NIV)
A good name is better than fine perfume, and the day of death better than the day of birth.

Song of Solomon 1:3 (NIV)
Pleasing is the fragrance of your perfumes; your name is like perfume poured out. No wonder the young women love you!

1 Timothy 5:1-2 (NIV)
Do not rebuke an older man harshly, but exhort him as if he were your father. Treat younger men as brothers, older women as mothers, and younger women as sisters, with absolute purity.

Chapter Five
Trading Spaces: Visitation

Now may our God and Father himself and our Lord Jesus clear the way for us to come to you. 1 Thessalonians 3:11 (NIV)

Visitation Schedules

L iving-in-step means navigating and conquering visitation schedules. By the time we married, our visitation schedules were purposely synchronized to have our children at the same time on weekends and holidays. Each January, we calibrated our electronic calendars and penciled in "kid weekends," so as we made plans for the year, all activities could be planned around our visitation days. This arrangement certainly had its advantages. Having our kids at the same time meant we could encourage our children to build relationships with one another, and our stepchildren could see us both in a parenting role. With this schedule, we had two weekends a month with a house full and two weekends when we could have some much needed couple time. Having the same weekend visitation schedule seemed to be the perfect arrangement for us, and we did not deviate from it unless one of the bio-parents had different plans.

According to the Stepfamily Foundation, predictability and consistency are critical for stepfamilies. When there is inconsistency, we do more psychological harm than good. When parents and children understand their roles and know what is expected of them, the family can operate as a successful unit. If your husband is the noncustodial parent, it is vital to establish clearly what the visitation schedule will be regardless if it is every other weekend, once a month, or during the summer. Plan the schedules in advance and communicate them by writing them down on a calendar; stick to them, and be on time. Many movies have presented the father in a bad light by showing sad, disappointed kids sitting in the window waiting expectantly for their dad, who either shows up late or not at all. Although visitation weekends may be tough on you as a stepmom, it is important that the children spend time with their father.

A Standard Weekend Visit

From the very start, both of us were excited about our weekend visits from Bobby's children. My vision of the perfect family weekend was a loving home where everyone felt welcomed, valued, and happy. Preparations began on Thursdays by synchronizing schedules and activities and making sure bedrooms were ready. Meals were coordinated, and the cabinets and refrigerators were well stocked.

Bobby picked up the kids on Friday evening no later than 6:00 PM, and I made plans to be home by the time he arrived. A sure way to enhance the relationship with your stepchildren is to create arrival rituals. My ritual was to greet them at the door excited about their arrival. Once the garage door went up, I met them at the back door with hugs and kisses. I assisted with getting bags and helping them to get settled in their rooms if needed.

I was happy and proud to be "Janice the Super-Mom" or the "Proverbs 31 Woman" that "watches over the affairs of her household." It was important to me that I did everything in my power to make them feel comfortable in our home. In addition, it was vital that my husband knew I loved and cared for his children. I really didn't want him to worry about anything but enjoying our time with his children.

Our first few months together were January and February, and we had a typical, cold Kansas winter. Most of our activities were confined to indoors. Occasionally, we were blessed with great weather and the kids played outside, or we took a Saturday or Sunday evening walk together. Friday nights commonly included selecting a variety of movies from Blockbuster and watching them together. There were additional indoor activities like play station, X-Box, or other games the kids enjoyed. We purchased a family computer and placed it in a central location for everyone's use. It was available for doing homework, playing games or, simply surfing the internet. We also encouraged Bobby's kids to bring over their favorite toys or games.

Saturdays were fun, lazy days if no one had activities on the schedule; however, these days were few and far between. Bobby's children were extremely active in non-school related sports, which meant many of the games were on Saturdays. Jamie was involved in basketball at the Salvation Army and had games on Saturday mornings, sometimes as early as 8:00. Even though my Saturday plans included sleeping in, we would get up early, load up the Cadillac, and go to Jamie's games to be supportive as a family. During football season, Bobby's youngest son Brandon had junior league games. I wasn't much of a football fan, but endured the rain or the cold to cheer him on. A few weekends consisted of church activities, but we tried to do them together with the goal of including everyone who wanted to participate.

Sundays

Sunday mornings were hectic because we had to get up early to get everybody in and out of the bathroom, and ready for church. After a few episodes of forgetting to pack church clothes, we double checked clothing on Friday when unpacking to make sure everything was there. Socks and shoes were often forgotten. My routine consisted of waking up a few hours before everyone else, to get myself ready and to prepare my famous Sunday morning breakfast which consisted of cinnamon rolls, blueberry muffins, and bacon. Cooking breakfast on Sunday mornings was a tradition and trick I learned from my own mom. As a child, waking up to the smell of homemade waffles kept me and my sisters from complaining about having to get up early on Sunday mornings.

Simultaneously while cooking breakfast, I also prepared Sunday dinner and put something in the oven to slow cook while we were at church. Sunday school started at 9:00, so by 8:45, we had to be on our way. On First Sundays, Bobby and I had an early meeting at church and sometimes took children with us, or we came back home quickly to pick them up before Sunday school started. Thank God, Aaron eventually got his driver's license and his own car. He was able to help out significantly.

After church, we returned home and couldn't wait to get out of our church clothes. As everyone else retreated to their rooms, I put the finishing touches on our Sunday dinner. Being a pastor, Bobby had a full day and following service had loose ends to tie up, so he often arrived home after us. I enjoyed Sunday dinners, so I really didn't mind doing most of the cooking. I didn't realize how much food it took to feed a large family, but Bobby helped me make the adjustment by buying in large quantities. The girls set the table, the table was spread, Bobby blessed the food, and everyone recited a scripture.

The rest was history as I watched the food disappear quickly. My kids were never big eaters, so it was great to see children enjoying the meal. Sometimes, I thought the boys were engaged in eating contests to see who could eat the most food. During dinner and other meals, we talked about whatever the subject of the day was and encouraged everyone to participate in the conversation. If one child was not engaged, Bobby and I pulled him or her into the dialogue by asking him or her a question.

Bobby's kids were taught at a very young age to thank the cook for the meal, particularly if they were visiting; therefore, at every meal I was usually thanked and complimented on a particular dish or the entire meal by each child one at a time. One said, "Thank you" or "This is good," and the others chimed in. We expected everyone to remain at the table until we were finished eating. Occasionally, when we had adult visitors, the kids were excused from the table early. Once the meal was over, everyone knew to clean his or her plate, assist with loading the dishwasher, and wiping down the table. I usually stored the leftovers. After the meal, our children were free to do whatever they wanted. They often retreated to their rooms to watch television or take a nap. At 5:30 on Sunday evenings, the Love kids began preparations to go home. At 5:45, we said our goodbyes, loaded the car, and returned them to the bio-mom's house by the required time which was 6:00.

Home Alone

We did our best to focus our weekends around the kids' visit, but of course life had to go on. Bobby and I attempted to restrict our non-kid friendly activities, but some events including work or church, demanded our attendance on a Saturday or Sunday. It was satisfactory if only one of us had to be gone, but occasionally both of us had to be absent from the home. If that were the case, we placed my son Aaron in charge until we returned. This arrangement worked well because Aaron was in high school and everyone looked up to him and listened to him.

During one of our outings, Bobby's cell phone began to ring. He didn't answer it, and it rang again and again. He looked at the caller ID and realized the calls were coming from our house, so we were alarmed. My kids usually did not call me unless it was an emergency, so we were anxious. When Bobby called the house, Jamie answered wanting to know when we were coming home. He informed her of our estimated time of arrival and asked if everything was alright. I double checked to see if everything was okay by calling Aaron from my cell phone. He assured me that everyone was fine and wasn't aware of Jamie's calls to us.

Jamie making numerous calls while we were gone became a pattern, whenever both of us or just Bobby was away from the house. Once we realized it was Jamie, we tried to ignore Bobby's ringing cell phone. On a few occasions, when Jamie became distressed, she convinced my daughter Aiden to call me on my cell phone. When we didn't answer, Jamie made other calls, including to the bio-mom and informed her that we had left them home alone and that she was scared. The last thing I wanted was Jamie calling her entire network when we were out of the house, so I asked Bobby to speak with Jamie about the frequent phone calls. Bobby talked with her and discovered that this was typical behavior for Jamie. She repeated the same behavior at the bio-mom's house whenever she was absent. I wanted to intervene and discipline Jamie, but knew it was not my place to change the behavior if it was acceptable to her parents. I did however, remind Aiden of our rules about calling when I was away from home.

Eat, Drink, and Be Merry

According to the Stepfamily Foundation, the family meal is the altar of the family. It is the setting for teaching values, ethics, and a vision of self and the world. Because it was a great opportunity for our family to spend time together, we carefully planned our meals. We knew everyone's favorite foods and sometimes prepared their recommendations. It was important to Bobby to have an abundance of food whenever anyone was hungry. After the meal was concluded, Bobby kept the food available just in case someone wanted another round of feasting. Leaving the food out was different for me because my custom had been that once the meal was over and the dishwasher was loaded, the food was put in the refrigerator, and the kitchen was closed.

As I mentioned before, I wasn't used to cooking for a large family, and Bobby used to tease me about preparing food in portions. Leftovers had never been my favorite, so I prepared what I knew would be eaten in a single setting. Preparing portions was also my way of managing my weight and attempting not to waste food. Bobby loved seeing a full refrigerator and thought I kept mine a little too barren. It didn't take me long to realize that Bobby's children had inherited his large appetite, and they too had a great appreciation for good food. They were all tall and didn't have to worry about counting calories. Eventually, my children and I grew to embrace having an abundance of food in the refrigerator.

In our first home, there was a breakfast bar in the kitchen. It had two barstools and was often used for eating quick meals or when eating alone. For family meals, there was a table that sat six in the formal dining room. The dining room furniture included a china cabinet, a table with an extension leaf, and six chairs, two of them with arms. When there were only three of us, I removed two of the chairs and the extension leaf. I considered meal time special and required we eat together as a family in the formal dining room. Sitting down at the table and eating together provided an opportunity for me to connect with my children. All of our family meals were served in the dining room. I sat at the head of the table opposite Aaron with Aiden in the middle. This seating placed Aaron in a "man of the house position."

As Bobby and I were dating, my memory is limited as to all of us sitting down together eating a meal. Most of our joint meals consisted of Friday night pizza, and the kids were allowed to eat wherever they wanted except for the bedrooms. Often the boys sat at the breakfast bar, the girls ate in the dining room, and Bobby and I ate in the den. While we were dating, Bobby often ate dinner at his parents' house when he had his children. In preparation of our marriage and being excited about having family meals together, we rearranged the dining room by moving the china cabinet, adding the extension leaf and the additional chairs. We didn't discuss seating arrangements for our everyday household, but I was excited about having Bobby seated at the head of the table. Not wanting to create issues for Aaron, I chose not to move him and chose for me the seat closest to Bobby. This pattern also kept Aiden between Aaron and me. Bobby sat at the head of the table, I sat to his left, Aiden sat to my left, and Aaron sat at the other end of the table. See Illustration below.

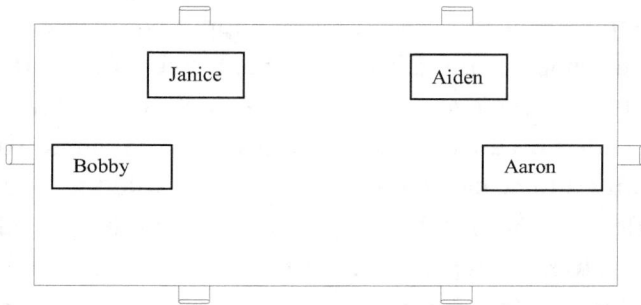

Janice		Aiden
Bobby		Aaron

During visitation weekends the table was set to accommodate seven. We only had six chairs so we brought in a folding chair from the card table set. Because the chair was awkward and smaller, I volunteered to sit in it. We placed it in the spot closest to the kitchen, which was also closest to Bobby (see illustration).

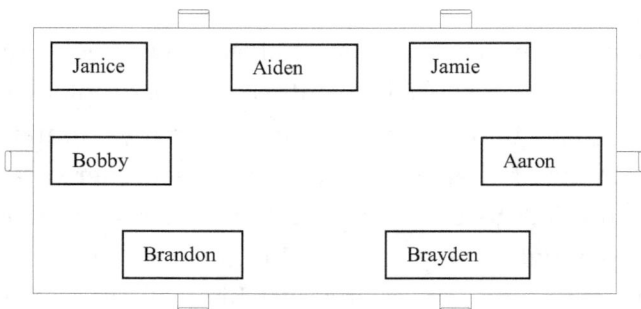

Janice	Aiden	Jamie
Bobby		Aaron
	Brandon	Brayden

Traditional table seating for families usually places the father and mother at the heads of both ends of the table (king and queen model) with the children in the middle. This seating arrangement had been used by both of us in our previous marriages and was considered optimal for families. In our new arrangement, the extra chair caused us to deviate from this model. We focused on not wanting to put any of the kids in the "extra" chair. I never thought in my wildest dreams that seating arrangements would make such a difference in attitudes and behaviors before, during, and after meals.

Routinely for dinner meals, the girls assisted with setting the table and then returned to their rooms until the food was placed on the table, and the meal was announced. Once supper was declared ready, I noticed Jamie rushed to the table and sat in the seat that had been assigned to Aiden. Whenever Jamie sat in Aiden's seat, it created problems for Aiden because she wanted to sit next to me. It was clear that Aiden wanted to be close to me, and Jamie wanted to be close to Bobby. It made sense after Bobby explained that in their prior home, Jamie sat closest to him. Because she was accustomed to sitting next to Bobby, she felt uncomfortable sitting between my children, Aaron and Aiden. Once we discovered the dynamics around the seating arrangements for the girls, we switched Jamie and Brandon. Then meals became more enjoyable for everyone. It's funny how such small things can make a major difference.

Summer Visitation

The standard visitation schedule allows at least two weeks during the summer with the non-custodial parent, so we made plans early for when we would have Bobby's children and when my children were to spend time with their father. My philosophy on summer vacation was that children needed to stay busy and have structured activities. Aaron was old enough to stay home by himself, but I didn't want him sitting around sleeping, eating, and watching television all day or getting into trouble out of boredom. Before marrying Bobby, I often sent for my nephew who was close in age to Aaron to stay with us for the summer. They kept one another company and out of trouble. One summer, I hired a school teacher to come by and pick them up a few days a week and take them swimming, to the library, mall, swimming, or whatever else they wanted to do. Aiden was not old enough to stay at home with them, so I typically enrolled her in a summer day-care program. Bio-mom made the summer plans for Bobby's children with the exception of the weeks they were with us.

One summer, I had the opportunity to sign our youngest three up for a free summer camp in close proximity to my job. Families who lived or worked in the corridor had the first option of signing their kids up for the summer program. I put our applications in early, and all three of them were selected to participate. The classes were divided by age groups, so all three would be at different locations, but they were just down the street from one another. My daughter Aiden had attended the year before and was familiar with the program. We were excited because they would all be participating in structured programs, and the real bonus was we didn't have to pay anything. I was proud of myself for helping Bobby give his children options for the summer. It would be a sacrifice for me to leave earlier in the morning, but I was doing it for the kids' benefit. The programs started at 8:00 in the morning, so we had to leave the house no later than 7:15 to get everyone where they were going. I negotiated a slight change in my work schedule in order to execute our plan.

We made arrangements with the bio-mom for Brandon and Jamie to stay with us during the weeks of the program and to maintain the same weekend schedule. If for some reason, they stayed at the bio-mom's house, she dropped them off in the morning by 7:15. We structured bedtimes, activities, and bathing so everything ran smoothly. Our couple prayer time ritual included the kids during the months they participated in the program.

Each morning, we loaded the car, drove across the state line, and I delivered each one to his or her destination, signed them in, and arrived at work early. I left work early, picked them up, and returned home. During our drive, the kids talked about their day and upcoming field trips they were excited about. If it had been particularly hot on any given day, they fell asleep during the thirty minute drive. By the time we made it home, Bobby had dinner started, and everybody could rehash the day's experience. The first week went smoothly. Everyone adjusted nicely and appeared to be enjoying the summer program and our routines. There were a few complaints about the program lunches, but overall everyone seemed happy.

At the end of the second week, Bobby's kids went home for the weekend. When they returned on Sunday evening, Jamie had a different attitude about the program, and no longer wanted to participate. We encouraged her and reminded her of the fun she had talked about. The next few days brought on a huge behavior change in Jamie. After we arrived home in the evenings, she began to cry, telling us that she didn't want to go to the program anymore. The crying became intense, so we permitted her to telephone the bio-mom so she too could encourage Jamie that she was going to be okay and to stick with the plan. The crying soon led to sobbing for the rest of the evening. After a full week of Jamie crying and saying she didn't want to go to the camp and wanted to go home, we conceded and decided Jamie could return home for the rest of the summer. I didn't take Jamie's behavior personally nor suppose that she didn't want to be with us, I believed that she truly missed her mom and preferred a more carefree summer. Brandon finished out the summer with us.

My children often spent a week or two weeks with their bio-dad during the summer. I appreciated the break and encouraged the children to enjoy the time with their father. Bobby and I valued having the house to ourselves. For Bobby's children, we consistently planned a two week visit with us. The first week would typically be the second week of June when we had Bible school. Later in the summer before they went back to school, Bobby selected another week for his kids to visit. If our finances permitted, Bobby planned a getaway just for them without me. I was thrilled for them to spend some time together and encouraged them to have fun. I was an expert at finding great vacations in the area and assisted Bobby with making travel arrangements. My children also enjoyed having the house to ourselves, particularly Aiden, because we would eat out almost every day.

What's Mom Doing While We Are Gone?

During my single years, I considered my "kid free" weekends a special treat. I was happy my children enjoyed visits to their father's house every other weekend and other special occasions he wanted them to visit. While they were gone, I had the luxury of doing things for myself and enjoying some much needed "me" time. In the beginning, I assured my children I would be okay while they were gone and that I enjoyed having quiet time. To make it convenient for the bio-dad to manage Aiden's hair, I combed it in a low maintenance style. I was looking forward to the day when he remarried so that he could have some help with Aiden's full head of hair.

Because I appreciated my time alone so much, I assumed during the weekends we had the children, the bio-mom would also appreciate her time alone. What we observed was that Jamie seemed particularly worried about what her mom was doing when they were visiting us. She frequently commented on needing to check on her mom to make sure she was okay. We learned later that the children did not feel comfortable leaving their mother home by herself. She was used to having them around and had not yet gained an appreciation for a quiet house.

While the kids were at our house, the bio-mom occupied her time with family activities. As mentioned previously, the bio-mom's extended family was very large, and it wasn't uncommon for their family to get together during the week or on weekends to go to the movies, have birthday celebration dinners and parties, anniversaries parties, or anything else that deserved celebrating. Whenever Jamie called to check on her mom, she asked what she was doing and where she was going. If she was doing something that sounded exciting, Jamie felt like she was missing out on all of the fun. Jamie loved being on the go and around people; it was part of her temperament as my husband informed me. It drove her nuts to be sitting at our house doing nothing when her mom was out having fun with the extended family.

Brandon really enjoyed staying at our home and often asked to stay after the weekend was over. During a Memorial Day weekend, Brandon requested to extend his weekend stay with us. I often used holidays to catch up on house cleaning, so we didn't have much planned. Sunday evening, we went to Blockbuster to pick up videos to watch late into the night. Upon arriving, we ran into the bio-mom also picking up videos. While in the store, we encouraged Brandon to say hello. We completed our purchase and made a few more stops before returning home.

After getting into the car, I noticed a change in Brandon's demeanor. He appeared overly sad about something. After we arrived home, I mentioned it to Bobby, and he agreed he had noticed the change as well. He talked with Brandon alone and found he was sad because the bio-mom had told him they were going swimming on Monday, but because he was with us, he was not going to be able to go. One thing I knew about Brandon was that he was always eager to go swimming. We knew our plans to watch movies all night and then be lazy on the holiday no longer seemed enjoyable to him. I'm sure Brandon didn't want to hurt our feelings by asking to go home, so he stuck it out. I almost felt guilty enough to let him off the hook and ask him if he wanted to go home, but I didn't want to interfere and give Bobby the impression the bio-mom had won.

Disneyland Dad

We soon found ourselves trying to compete with the bio-mom by making sure the kids had something fun to do while at our home. Having a bunch of activities planned for the weekend was abnormal for our household, so whenever we tried to entertain them by coming up with a bunch of activities, we were off balance. My kids loved staying at home all day, but his kids began to complain that our house was boring because they didn't get to go a lot of places. We tried to convince them that the time with us was more important; however, we were no match for all the activities the bio-mom and her extended family participated in.

A common mistake made by newly divorced fathers is they become "Disneyland Dads." These are fathers who feel powerless to perform and overlook their fathering responsibilities by packing the weekend with fun activities and spending money. It is often done out of guilt for not spending enough time with the children during the week and/or the divorce itself. Guilt creates overindulgence and can lead to shame, which inhibits discipline and action altogether. This behavior leads to the children having unrealistic expectations about their time with their father. Rather than building a relationship on being together and spending quality time, it is replaced by activities that make the weekend entertaining.

Fortunately, Bobby did not become a Disneyland dad. His weekend schedule prevented him from attempting to use his time with them as a way to make up to them. Time and money did not permit him to appease them by going everywhere they wanted to go and buying whatever they wanted. Before you marry someone with children, be observant of how your future mate spends time with his children and how much money is spent on entertainment and possessions. If you witness Disneyland activity, pray for guidance on how to help him understand this phenomenon, but be careful you do not accuse him of having guilt and neglecting his parental duties. Remember, the kids love it when he spends lots of money on them and takes them to fun places. Encourage him to make changes before you are married so that you are not blamed for the changes. While you are at it, make sure you have not become a Disneyland mom exhibiting similar behavior. Remember divorced parents are often more lenient.

I Don't Want to Come Over

The younger boys, Brayden and Brandon, enjoyed coming to our house, but as time went by Jamie did not. During visits, Jamie asked if she could call home to check on the bio-mom. We allowed her to call whenever she wanted to, but encouraged her to limit the calls to just saying hello and goodnight. We knew she and her mom were close, and Jamie didn't like being away from her. The bio-mom had always encouraged Jamie to have a good time at our house, but to call her if she were unhappy or missed her. The call usually began by just checking to see how mom was doing. We didn't eavesdrop in on the calls, but on more than one occasion Jamie's voice was raised, and we overheard her asking, "I don't want to be over here; can you come and pick me up?" My assumption was that the bio-mom had told her that she would not come and pick her up because crying and sobbing often followed. Bobby began to monitor the calls to ensure they didn't turn into crying sessions. Despite our efforts, the emotional conversations with the bio-mom led to the same conclusion: Jamie wanted to go home.

One weekend the behavior became so extreme, it resulted in a crying temper tantrum that was elevated a few more notches in volume. I wasn't used to hearing a child yell at an adult and asked Bobby why they allowed her to yell and scream like that? I wanted to reprimand her and tell her she could not talk to the bio-mom that way. It was pretty obvious this behavior was not going to end any time soon, so I conceded and asked Bobby to take her home to the bio-mom. It didn't take long for Jamie to figure out how to make it happen yet again. Whenever we failed to have something fun planned for the weekend, the "I don't want to come over" conversation began. I was concerned as to why she didn't want to spend time with us and encouraged Bobby to spend some time talking with her. Jamie's list of complaints included: early bedtimes, chores, Aiden's possessions, me being mean to her, and Bobby not listening to her and always taking my side.

Being the problem solver I am, I tried to help the circumstances by calling the bio-mom to see what I could do to help Jamie feel more comfortable in our home, so that she would desire to visit. The bio-mom informed me Jamie did not like coming to our house because we did not listen to her. Jamie also wanted to spend some time with her father alone, and she didn't want him taking my side all of the time. She also mentioned that Jamie did not like it when we left them at home when we had things to do. The other grievance was that we didn't do anything fun. In essence, she confirmed everything Jamie had told Bobby. She didn't offer any solutions, and the problem continued to escalate. The behavior continued to the point of our weekend visits becoming agonizing. She cried when Bobby picked her up, and our weekends were fretful. Throughout the weekend, the calls to the bio-mom continued.

It finally got to the point I felt we needed to do something to resolve this dilemma. Bobby and I discussed whether or not it was fair to oblige Jamie to come over and concluded if she didn't want to come to our house, we were no longer going to force her to come. I suggested Jamie begin to notify us before the weekend if she wanted to come over; otherwise, she would stay at home. This decision may not have been the right one, but we needed peace in our home during visitation weekend. Our desire was that our decision would result in the bio-mom encouraging Jamie's visits to our home. By her remaining at home, Jamie would infringe upon the bio-mom's time, and she would realize her part in supporting this behavior. Also, we hoped by having her to request to come over it would change Jamie's behavior in our home. For the next five months, Jamie did not participate in weekend visitation. It wasn't until the Christmas holiday when the bio-mom had plans of her own that Jamie planned to come over for a weekend visit. Following the holidays, her visits resumed.

The other approach our children used on occasion was arranging to spend the night with a friend during our weekend visitation. We didn't have any extra beds on kid weekend, so we rarely allowed the kids to have friends sleep over. We agreed this wasn't always fair to the kids, but we didn't want to crowd the house anymore or expose our chaos to other children. Our compromise was to allow them to spend the night occasionally with one of their friends particularly if we knew the parents. When we sensed our children trying to avoid our household, the requests were denied. Not always a popular decision. When desperate, the kids would try to put their friend's parent on the phone to convince us it was okay for them to stay over.

Part-Time Parenting

Experience has left me with the conclusion that it is more difficult to build a relationship with stepchildren when you spend only four days per month with them. Staying for the weekend seems more like a sleepover, and establishing a true family model is difficult. Many other stepmoms have struggled in this area and have lost hope of developing bonds with their stepchildren. Custodial parents have much more time to parent than those who see their children only every other weekend. Weekends were a real struggle for us, and we found ourselves bewildered on what we could do to make things better.

Somewhere in year two or three, I accepted the fact that Bobby's kids wanted to spend time with their father alone, and my presence was preventing them from doing so. I really enjoyed staying at home on Saturdays, but wanted Bobby to have some private time without my interference. On occasion, I changed my Saturday routine, and Aiden and I went out for most of the day. We slept in, ate breakfast and left around mid-day and returned in the evening before or after dinner. Bobby and his kids seemed to appreciate our absence as long as Aiden and I didn't do anything too exciting during our time out of the house. Sometimes, our outings created greater dissention because it looked as if we were having too much fun. As a result of me and Aiden's outings, more requests were made of Bobby to go more places on Saturdays. Aiden and I enjoyed being at home, therefore I was happy to trade places and stay at home with Aiden while Bobby and his kids were out and about.

Doing activities with our children separately seemed to work for the kids, but Bobby and I began to feel like we were living separate lives on visitation weekends. We grabbed quick moments alone and reminded ourselves it was just for the weekend. Our time alone was limited and different. We were normally a very affectionate couple, but displayed very little affection or intimacy when his kids were around. Based on Bobby's behavior, I sensed that our closeness made his children feel uncomfortable. He never said anything, but I could just tell. His actions spoke much louder than his words.

Bobby's emotions during visitation were torn between excitement and anxiety. He was excited to spend time with his kids because he missed them greatly. Caring for his kids for a few days helped him deal with the guilt of not living with them full time. Our uneasiness usually started on Thursday when we began to discuss the weekend's activities. The closer it came to Friday, Bobby's excitement to see the kids began to pair with my anxiety. It wasn't uncommon for us to argue about something on Thursday night or Friday because of our anxiety levels. Sensing my stress level, Bobby would go into overdrive and become nervous. He transferred his anxiety to his kids by informing them how they needed to behave when they came over. He reminded them to speak, not be too loudly, and say please and thank you. During the entire weekend, everyone was on pins and needles and tiptoeing around each other. It was impossible for anyone to be natural.

Even as a part-time stepparent, always keep in the back of your mind the possibility of your stepchildren making your home their permanent home. In Rev. Steve and Donna Houpe's book, *Becoming One Family: Bringing Blended Families Together,* they offer guidelines for the new family to follow to be successful. According to them, "Identifying and communicating expectations is the first step toward a pleasant transition from visits to permanently becoming one family" (Houpe and Houpe 2008, 117). Based on what we experienced on our visitation weekends, the thought of full-time step parenting was frightening.

You Can't Fix Them in a Weekend

It didn't take long for me to determine that Bobby's children exhibited certain behaviors that I did not approve of, and I made it my mission to help him parent them with the intention of changing unwanted behaviors. I agonized that their behavior was a reflection of my parenting skills or my inability to control them. I assumed that how they looked or acted when they were residing at our home was a reflection of me. If they fell asleep in church, it was my fault because I let them stay up all night, or if they wore inappropriate clothes, they did so because I let them.

I do admit that I am a control freak and feel parents should strongly influence their children's behavior. There were times I reprimanded his children for falling asleep in church or doing other things that I did not approve of. I complained to Bobby on several occasions regarding his daughter's clothing choices. My idea of fixing the situation was to purchase what I considered acceptable clothing for Jamie to wear to church when she was at our house.

I could probably create a long list of things I wanted to help his kids do differently; as I'm sure he could do the same. As I found myself complaining to Bobby, I realized I was being judgmental about his children and the way that he and the bio-mom had raised them. I had to finally accept that living-in-step meant not criticizing how their former household operated, but allowing him to parent his children the best way he knew how in those few days they were with us. I had to learn to let things go and look the other way so I would not be constantly trying to change who they were when they were with us. I was much more relaxed (at least I think so) when I quit trying to fix whatever I thought they needed to do differently.

Couple Strength

With such a large stepfamily, it was crucial for us to have some couple time alone. Living-in-step can create a huge amount of stress on your marriage, so it is vital to spend time together without the children. We were fortunate in that we were able to accomplish this goal two weekends a month. As I look back, those weekends became our refuge to strengthen our love for one another and to communicate our needs in a secure environment. We were able to have some down time to help us weather the storms.

The Stepfamily foundation refers to a term called "Couple Strength." It is the commitment to each other and the commitment to learning how to partner in the marriage. The couple must remain steadfast to hold on to the vision of the kind of relationship they want and work towards strengthening the marriage. We strongly believed in this concept, and as an outreach to other couples, we developed a monthly marriage group in our church called Couple Strength to assist other couples in building strong marriages.

During our weekends, we celebrated by having a romantic weekend for two. Our Friday nights alone were referred to as date night. On Thursday evening, we eagerly made plans for our precious two days alone, deciding what to eat and whether to cook at home or go out on a date. Most often we preferred to stay home and have our favorite Friday dinner, which was Bobby's famous steak and shrimp. Not wanting to be disturbed, we turned off our cell phones and checked caller ID on our home phone if we received calls. Our goal was to spend time together to strengthen one another and our marriage. Our alone time was critical for our sanity, and it gave us the time we needed as a newlywed couple to continue to build upon our foundation.

As I close this chapter, it may seem that Jamie gets a bad rap as her name comes up a little more than the others particularly when describing their behavior. In actuality, Jamie had the most difficult adjustment to living-in-step mainly because she experienced greater conflict of loyalty issues. When she visited our home, she did not like being away from the bio-mom and felt guilty about trying to have a relationship with me. Much of her emotional turmoil she could not verbalize as a child, so she often acted out. In addition, she missed living with her dad and craved a stronger connection to him, but I was in the way. I encouraged Bobby to spend more private time with Jamie so they could create a lasting bond and their own private memories. I also discovered the stepmother-stepdaughter relationship is the most difficult of all step affiliations. Jamie and I had it really tough in the early years. Although I did not appreciate the drama, I learned a lot about myself and eventually Jamie. The good news is that Jamie and I now have a great relationship and have even considered going on a tropical vacation together, just the two of us.

Stepmom Survival Tips

1. Build Couple Strength by planning time alone with your spouse.
2. Always prepare for non-custodial visitation. Know all schedules in advance.
3. Plan your calendar around visitation. Don't plan your visitation around your calendar.
4. Be consistent in following visitation rules and rituals.
5. Know that visitation can be emotionally tough on everyone involved.
6. Always allow for privacy and time with the bio-parent.
7. If the visit is extremely difficult, get away for a little while to deal with your emotions.
8. If a child does not want to visit a bio-parent, have a discussion with the bio-parent and the child to encourage the desire to visit.
9. Don't try to fix or change children during the visit.
10. Prepare emotionally for visitation and take time to recover after the visit.

Helpful Scriptures

Amos 3:3
Can two walk together, except they be agreed?

Colossians 4:5 (NIV)
Be wise in the way you act toward outsiders; make the most of every opportunity.

Philemon 1:22 (NIV)
And one thing more: Prepare a guest room for me, because I hope to be restored to you in answer to your prayers.

Exodus 23:9 (NIV)
Do not oppress an alien; you yourselves know how it feels to be aliens, because you were aliens in Egypt.

2 Corinthians 2:1 (NIV)
So I made up my mind that I would not make another painful visit to you.

1 Peter 4:9 (NIV)
Offer hospitality to one another without grumbling.

Chapter Six
Christmas Comes But Once a Year: Annual Events

His sons used to take turns holding feasts in their homes, and they would invite their three sisters to eat and drink with them. Job 1:4-5 (NIV)

Family Traditions

We had pretty much gotten used to visitation, and our weekends soon became standard with a few exceptions. Just as you get into a rhythm, along comes holidays, with additional nuances for a family living-in-step. Traditional families often establish norms for holidays and special events, such as birthdays, Mother's Day, Father's Day, Christmas, Easter, Fourth of July, wedding anniversaries, and other holidays. I looked forward to these occasions because they usually involved food and fellowship. Given that these occasions occur the same time each year, there is plenty of time to plan accordingly. Living-in-step means trying to bring together two or more family traditions and attempting to establish new ones. Often, these events hold special memories in the lives of families; therefore, stepfamilies must be sensitive to children who would prefer "the way we used to do things." I will discuss our experiences for the most crucial annual events in our family. You may want to add to this list while making plans for your stepfamily.

Birthdays

I.   Bobby's Birthday

Bobby's birthday is in September which is a perfect time of year, particularly because of the fabulous weather. Also, he is the only one in our immediate families to have a birthday during that month. Bobby is a giver and isn't very good at asking for what he wants. As pastor, he mails all of his church members an annual birthday card with a two dollar bill in it. Our members, particularly the youth, get a kick out of getting the two dollar bill. He cares deeply about the birthdays of others, but he doesn't like to make a big deal about his. It is always a challenge to figure out what kind of gift he wants. After being married for several years, I encourage everyone to purchase something related to golf, it works every time.

When September arrived during our first year of marriage, my idea was to do something very special for him. A small family celebration with his parents and all of our children during visitation weekend sounded like a great idea. I called Bobby's older children, Brody and Janae, who were both away at college, and invited them to celebrate with us. Brody was almost three hours away and indicated that he couldn't afford to make the trip. He agreed to join us after I offered help with gas money. Janae was closer and made plans to attend, but warned me that she would be running late. Bryson had already relocated out of state and would not be able to attend.

On the day of the celebration, I left work early, stopped by Kansas City's famous Gates Barbeque, and picked up a couple of rib platters with all of the fixings. Bobby arrived shortly afterwards with his kids followed by the arrival of his parents. He wasn't expecting his parents, so it turned out to be a great surprise to have us all together to celebrate his special day. He was particularly thrilled that Brody and Janae had come to celebrate with us. The food was plentiful and tasty, and the house was full of joy and laughter.

During the week, I had located the perfect birthday gift and bought a birthday card from myself and one for my kids to sign. For some reason, I assumed Bobby's kids were just as prepared. My assumption was based on my own traditions in which I assisted my children in making sure they celebrated their father's birthday. It came as a complete surprise to me when I realized Bobby's kids did not have a card for him. It felt awkward when my kids gave him something and his own kids did not. Guilt consumed me because I should have asked. Even with the omission, the night was a success and the older kids ended up staying at the house laughing and talking until 3:00 in the morning.

The second year was here before I knew it. Because his birthday came during the middle of the week, I decided just to make plans to take him to dinner. Bobby mentioned he had received several calls from Brody during the day mentioning that he was coming over later to pick up a bicycle stored at our house. Bobby was tickled because he thought it was Brody's way of trying to figure out what time he was going to be home and was planning a big surprise. I got home from work and found Brody at the house so I assumed that he was there because it was Bobby's birthday. I went upstairs to change clothes.

When I returned downstairs, Bobby said he was ready to go. I asked where Brody was and Bobby replied "He got the bicycle and left." We drove to the restaurant, but Bobby seemed very quiet. I thought for a moment that he was just reflecting on being another year older, but sensed something else was wrong. Finally, I asked him what Brody had done for his birthday. He shrugged his shoulders and said, "Nothing, yet."

I didn't understand, so I asked about the earlier visit. He kept reminding me the purpose of the visit had been to pick up the bicycle. I kept asking questions like, "Did he say anything about your birthday?" "Did he look like he was trying to plan something secretive?" We continued to believe that they were going to surprise him in a grand way later that evening and were waiting on us to get back home. By the time we returned home, there were no messages on his cell phone or the home answering machine. We couldn't figure out what had happened, so Bobby went to bed saddened that he had not received a birthday wish from any of his children. They must have forgotten.

A few days later Bobby received apologetic calls and belated birthday wishes. A few weeks later, a card came in the mail with all of their signatures. I never did ask him how he felt about what had happened, but I felt miserable. This was unusual behavior for his children because they usually made a big deal about birthdays and never seemed to forget one. They often helped other family members celebrate their birthdays on a grand scale. I wrestled with myself about whether or not to have a very firm conversation with at least one of them so that Bobby would never have to experience another unacknowledged birthday. Later on, Brody and I had a private conversation. I mentioned how disappointed Bobby was and reminded him that they should always do something for their father on his birthday. The more I thought about it, I assumed it may have been financial, so I assured him if money was an issue, I would provide assistance if needed.

From that point on, there was never again a forgotten birthday. On Bobby's 50th birthday, we had a big formal celebration and invited over a hundred guests. Now that the older kids are employed, they make a special effort to make their dad's birthday special. Occasionally, we celebrate his birthdays together, but I am okay with it if they want to do something for him without me.

II.   Children's Birthdays

My kids were much more fortunate than I was as a child. When they were younger, I always made a big event out of their birthdays. I excitedly planned themed parties at the location of their choice. It was not uncommon to spend several hundred dollars for the party and gifts. Following my divorce, their father and I continued to have joint birthday parties. We agreed on the party details including what gifts to purchase and evenly split the costs. The year Bobby and I married, my daughter Aiden decided to have a slumber party. I informed the bio-dad of her wishes and invited him over for pizza and cake. He accepted the invitation, and he and Bobby took turns taking pictures. Everyone got along fine and Aiden had a great birthday celebration.

After moving to the Kansas City area, my son Aaron refused to have any more birthday parties. He rationalized that all of his friends lived in Oklahoma and he had no one to invite; therefore, his birthday celebrations consisted of the dinner of his choice and a few gifts. Whatever I did for my kids, Bobby went along with it, and I signed the card with both of our names. If a birthday fell on a kid weekend, we involved everyone.

After a few birthday parties, it became obvious to me that Aiden wanted to celebrate her birthday when the other kids weren't there. I had always limited the number of guests and now she had a step brother and sister whom I insisted she invite. In her mind, they were taking up slots reserved for her friends. Aiden in particular became very strategic about planning her parties.

Communication was not the best between Bobby and the bio-mom, so they were unable to plan joint activities for their children. Plans were often made to have some kind of celebration at her home. Bobby's children would inform him of the plans and ask if we were coming. They had an expectation that we would attend their birthday parties, but we were uncomfortable going to the bio-mom's home uninvited. We usually ended up purchasing gifts and made arrangements to deliver them on their birthdays.

During our first year together, I wanted to do something special for Jamie's birthday because she was having difficulty adjusting to our marriage. Her birthday fell on our weekend, so I agreed to host a slumber party at our home. We worked together and sent out invitations to some of her school friends. As the mothers of the guests called to RSVP, I explained that I was Jamie's stepmom and the party was going to be held at our house. It turned out to be a great little party, and all of the girls enjoyed themselves. Even Aiden seemed to have a good time because her best friend, who also happened to be Jamie's cousin, was present. Bobby was especially pleased because the parents allowed their daughters to come over to our house.

Before Brayden's sixteenth birthday, I called the bio-mom and asked her to meet me for lunch. In our discussion, I asked that we be included in birthday parties and other special events and that we would be more than happy to share half of the expenses. I suggested we find neutral places to have the parties. She agreed to work together, but Brayden's birthday came and went, and we had separate celebrations. I suggest always trying to work with the bio-parents to celebrate children's birthdays as a solid unit as much as possible. Kids need to see the adults working together on their behalf. Parents working together can prevent the competition of trying to outdo one another.

III.   My Birthday

I grew up in a family where birthdays were celebrated at a minimum. My family tradition included Dad going to his favorite bakery and purchasing a birthday cake. Mom bought the birthday card, a small gift, and we celebrated as a family with cake and ice cream following dinner. I can't remember ever having a birthday party where I was allowed to invite my friends over, nor do I remember getting calls from extended relatives, such as aunts and uncles or grandparents. Birthdays were private events that we celebrated within our household.

I try not to make a big fuss about my birthday. My expectations are low and may include minimal activities from family members, such as a phone call, email, or text. Facebook has opened up a whole new realm, and now everyone knows when it is your birthday. I don't expect cards, but I usually receive birthday cards from my immediate family and closest friends. My sisters and I have a running family contest to see who can actually send each other's card on time. Every now and then, we drop the ball and may send a card a few months later than the birthday actually happens. In our opinion, whenever the card comes, it is much appreciated.

My birthday usually falls around the Martin Luther King holiday which is great because I get a day off work. Also in January, we celebrate our wedding anniversary and the birthdays of Bobby's mother and brother. The year we married, we held our wedding reception on my birthday, so I really didn't have any expectations. The following year we had just celebrated our anniversary with a trip to California, and I was still glowing. We spent a lot of money on Christmas and our anniversary trip, so I was hoping that Bobby wouldn't go out and try to do anything big for me. My birthday fell on a Sunday, so the church staff did something special for me as the first lady.

My kids were taught to plan ahead for birthdays and holidays. They usually acknowledged my birthday with a card and a gift that they would present first thing in the morning. Before marrying Bobby, the kids were used to seeking their dad's assistance to purchase something during the weekend they were visiting with him; therefore, when Bobby asked about what they wanted to do, they already had it taken care of. Gift wise, I wasn't hard to please. I liked gifts that were personal and not expensive, so when the kids asked, I always kept a few thoughts in the back of my mind to make it easier for them to do something simple and meaningful. Year two, Bobby and my kids were the only ones to acknowledge my birthday.

Bobby often felt guilty when his children did not do anything for me on or around my birthday. He would purchase something for them and have them sign a card. I didn't feel comfortable with this arrangement because he was doing all the work, so I asked him not to do it anymore. Now, I typically receive a text from almost everyone wishing me a happy birthday and a phone call. Bobby's oldest daughter Janae and I will usually have lunch sometime during the month. I am perfectly happy if my stepchildren remember my birthday and acknowledge it. Keeping my expectations low makes the smallest gestures great, and anything is appreciated.

Father's Day

We participated in the traditional holiday visitation schedule, which meant that regardless of the weekend visitation schedule, children are allowed to be with their father on Father's Day. Our first year, Bobby's kids were already at our house for visitation and no special arrangements had to be made. My kids and I had already bought Bobby and their bio-dad gifts, and my children presented their gift to Bobby before they left on Saturday night. When we woke up the next morning with just Bobby's kids in the house, they wished him a Happy Father's Day, but did not present a card or a gift. All of his children came to church, and I prepared an elaborate meal and invited his parents and brothers over. The kids were all present for dinner, but they still didn't have a card or a gift for their father. I don't think he really cared about either, but I could tell he was disappointed. As a result, I felt guilty and beat myself up emotionally because I should have checked with them in advance like I had done with my children. The following week, they did bring over a card signed by all of them.

Later, I spoke with Brody to ensure that Bobby would not experience discontent the next Father's Day. Year two was better, and they made sure to purchase something for him. Because Father's Day is on a Sunday, I always made plans to cook a big meal and invited Bobby's parents over to join us. I longed for the day when his kids would call me in advance and ask me to help them plan something for Father's Day. One or two years, I did receive a call the night before to inquire about what I had planned. I always assured them I was cooking a big dinner and everyone was invited.

The more I thought about what a great father Bobby was to his children, the more aggravated I became that they didn't make a big deal about Father's Day like they did for the bio-mom on Mother's Day. One year, the younger ones did not visit with us although it was our weekend; I had not heard from any of them. On Sunday morning, they all came to church and then just showed up at the house expecting a big dinner. Of course I had a Sunday meal, but resented being taken advantage of. I imagined the next year going to Oklahoma for the weekend and celebrating Father's Day with my dad. I could leave Bobby with a hundred bucks and tell him to take his kids out to dinner if they showed up. Of course, I never implemented this plan because I loved Bobby too much. Besides, I thought it would ruin his Father's Day sermon if he had to go to church disappointed on Father's Day. I rationalized the day only came around once a year and continued to prepare a big dinner for anyone who showed up. Sometimes I invited other couples to celebrate with us.

Although we had a full house on Father's Day, I always ended up feeling lonely. Once the meal was over and Bobby's parents left, the conversation usually shifted towards memories of Bobby and his kids past life together which did not include me. They enjoyed telling old stories and talking about how great things used to be. Most often, the reminiscing continued for three to four hours. Bobby loved seeing his children happy and engaging freely, and he relished those moments with them. It was great for them, so I embraced them for a short while and then retreated to our bedroom. Reading a book or watching a movie kept me busy while they fellowshipped. Later, my children came home and entertained me by telling me how their weekend went with their father.

One particular year, we experienced an outrageously busy week prior to Father's Day. Bobby had been out of town all week attending a meeting. When he returned on Friday night, we had to get up early on Saturday and drive out of town for a funeral. That Saturday evening, we were exhausted and got into the bed around 5:00 PM to take a quick nap. The quick nap turned into an early bedtime and suddenly it was 11:00 o'clock. Since it was so late, I refused to get up and go to the grocery store, purchase food, and begin preparations for the usual Father's Day meal. I decided that we would just go out for dinner. I informed Bobby I had not heard from his kids during the week, but I was sure they didn't mind going out for dinner.

I didn't sleep very well, and the more I thought about what to do for Father's Day, I decided Bobby would be most encouraged by having time to spend with his children without me being in the way. As long as he knew that I supported him as a father, he was happy. Once we got home from church, I recommended to Bobby that he go out with his children and enjoy a lovely dinner. I rationalized with him that Father's Day was about spending the day with your father. This option allowed them time together and helped the kids feel they were doing something for their father on their own. Everything worked out great. I got to spend some quiet time alone without having to do a lot of cooking, and was happy knowing that Bobby was having a great time with his kids.

Allowing Bobby to spend time alone with his children became our new model and is how we now celebrate Father's Day. Bobby's children select the restaurant and cover the costs of Bobby's meal. Bobby's father, affectionately known as Papa Love, will join them occasionally. If my father-in-law goes with them, I swing by and pick up my mother-in-law to give her a break, and she really values our outing. We may invite a few other ladies and make an event out of it. I no longer worry about making all the plans and being in the way of them celebrating Father's Day in a way that works for them.

Mother's Day

Having been divorced for several years, my kids already had Mother's Day figured out, or so I thought. In previous years, the bio-dad gave them money to purchase a gift for me and they did all of their shopping during their visitation with him. The year Bobby and I married, my kids presented me with a card only. This was fine with me, just different from the preceding years. The bio-dad had assumed because I was married, Bobby would take care of assisting my children with gift buying. I had already informed Bobby that my kids and their dad had a system, and he didn't need to worry about my kids. Again, I don't require much, but I guess my kids felt bad about not getting me a gift. I never said anything to them about it, nor did I mention anything to the bio-dad. When Father's Day arrived, I continued to do what I always did and assisted my children with purchasing a gift for the bio-dad. Following Father's Day, the bio-dad called to apologize, telling me that he would make sure that the kids got me something for Mother's Day.

Our first Mother's Day, Bobby was a nervous wreck. We had his children most of the weekend, and they were scheduled to go home on Sunday to be with their mother. Bobby wanted his kids to be excited about doing something for me, so he took them shopping on Saturday. When they came home later that night, I asked him what the kids had gotten for their mother. He informed me they had said nothing about buying something for her. He guessed that the older kids had taken care of the gift shopping. I encouraged him to double check with the older ones. Unfortunately, they had not done anything and Bobby became emotionally paralyzed. By then, it was already nine o'clock at night.

Feeling guilty because they had been shopping for me, I got dressed and went to the store to buy something for the bio-mom. By the time, I returned home, my feelings were hurt and I was already over Mother's Day. My idea of a wonderful Mother's Day was not spending Saturday evening trying to find the bio-mom a gift.

Bobby woke up early Sunday morning and began preparing dinner. After what I had been through the night before, having to go out and find the bio-mom a gift, Bobby was in a hurry to shower me with Mother's Day gifts before we went to church. His kids woke up with mixed emotions about wishing me a Happy Mother's Day because they had not spoken to their own mom yet. We had to remember this was the first time they had awakened on Mother's Day away from their mother. Bobby was saddened by their behavior and scolded them about how they should be nicer to me as their stepmother. The rest of the day was a blur, but I knew one thing: I didn't plan to go through another Mother's Day like the one I experienced our first year together.

Our second Mother's Day, Bobby wasn't feeling well, probably from being stressed about how the day would turn out after last year's fiasco. He made it through service, but was in no shape to do anything else except climb in the bed and go to sleep. I didn't worry about him preparing a meal and went and picked up something for us to eat. Bobby stayed in the bed, and my children and I had a nice meal together. When Bobby regained his strength later, we went by to visit his mother. I hadn't heard from any of Bobby's children, but later in the evening, Bobby's daughter Janae stopped by the house and brought me a candle. I was pleasantly surprised and appreciative of the gesture.

Most years, I receive a series of text messages in the morning and maybe a visit from Bobby's children late in the evening. I tried to take the pressure off of them and encourage them to spend time with their mother and grandmothers. While they embraced their biological family, I valued the time with my own children. Again, I keep my expectations low; therefore I am delighted by any gesture.

Christmas

Christmas has always been my favorite time of the year, and I make every effort to make it special for everyone. I decorate all of the living areas with some type of holiday cheer. Given that Bobby and I married on New Year's Day, we had plenty of time to think about our first Christmas together. Our visitation schedule allowed us to have the kids every other year for Christmas. If it was our year, we had them from Christmas Eve until 6:00 PM. Christmas Day. On alternating years, they arrived at our home after 6:00 p.m. Christmas Day. We were eager to celebrate because it was our first year together and we were beginning new traditions. It had been my custom to visit with my parents and siblings in Tulsa typically the weekend prior to Christmas. We planned to take all of our minor children to Tulsa so they could be acquainted with my loved ones. Then we would return and spend the entire week together, culminating on Christmas Day.

I eagerly made travel arrangements to travel to Oklahoma. Our last visit there, my sister was living in a much larger house and could accommodate all of us. Recently, she had moved into a one bedroom duplex, and my niece was living with her temporarily. My parents lived in a small three bedroom house and were unable to accommodate all of us. I did some research and found a two bedroom hotel suite with a kitchenette. A bedroom for Bobby and me and one for the girls, and the boys could sleep on the rollaway couch in the living area. My son Aaron was planning to stay with his cousins. I spent most of the week trying to reserve a mini-van or SUV to seat all eight of us, but was unsuccessful.

We survived the four hour drive in Bobby's Cadillac, (three in the front and four in the back) and made it to Tulsa safely. It's a good thing we weren't stopped by the law because there were not enough seat belts for everyone. We left Olathe late because my son Aaron had a basketball game, causing us to arrive late at night. We stopped at a grocery store and purchased late night snacks and breakfast items.

My family's annual Christmas celebration was more about getting together to fellowship than exchanging gifts. My three sisters and I habitually collaborated on a gift for our parents, but did not spend a lot of money on each other. Typical gifts were the most creative item we could find at the dollar store for no more than $5.00 per person. I telephoned my family in advance to let them know we were bringing all of the kids and to include them in the gift exchange. My kids knew from experience not to expect a lot of gifts from my extended family. When Bobby's kids opened their gifts, they were disappointed in the coloring books, socks, and other inexpensive items they received. The disappointment was all over their faces. My dad purchased an inexpensive toy musical instrument for Aiden that looked like a million bucks to Bobby's kids. It was very obvious by the way they clung to Bobby that they were not comfortable in the environment and were extremely disappointed in the gifts they had received. The ride back to Kansas City was quiet.

I loved being prepared for Christmas, so I make my list early and try to finish shopping no later than the first week of December. I began as early as November, informing my children of the Christmas budget and encouraged them to scan store sales catalogues, the internet, and television commercials to complete their wish lists. Their Christmas list had to include the name of the item, the price, and which store had the best price. I expected the documents be completed by Thanksgiving, so I could shop the sales on black Friday.

Bobby, on the other hand, is a Christmas Eve shopper. He doesn't like having to think about it all month, and he loves the pressure of being out there with the desperate crowd. The stores are often ready to close before he is finished shopping. He is accustomed to waking up early on Christmas Eve, putting his list together, leaving mid-morning, and returning after 10:00 at night. His final stop is Walgreens where he picks up extra wrapping paper and boxes. It is an adventure for him and gives him an adrenaline rush. His holiday gift buying system makes me a nervous wreck.

Prior to our first Christmas holiday together, I informed Bobby of my methodology and philosophy around Christmas shopping and the use of pre-planned lists. He liked my model and decided to try it with some variations. He asked the kids for lists and ended up with extensive lists with expensive items that we could not afford. It was too much trouble to have them revise their lists, so he said he would figure it out. I offered my assistance, but he said he was okay. I inquired about a date when we could shop together, but we were unable to coordinate our schedules. Looking at the calendar, I was nervously running out of time and decided to do the shopping for my kids alone.

On Christmas Eve, Bobby was still out shopping so I spent the afternoon and early evening with church friends. Every two hours, I called to check on Bobby's shopping expedition. When I arrived home, he was still out, so I began to wrap gifts. When Bobby finally came home from shopping, his feet were hurting, and he was tired and frustrated. The trunk of the car was stuffed with huge bags filled with everything imaginable. He dumped it all in the middle of our bedroom floor, and we sorted and boxed everything. I loved to wrap presents and usually created a different theme for each person. I wrapped them, stacked them, and then connected them with a lovely bow like the fancy Christmas wrapping seen in holiday advertisements. Bobby cut and taped paper and assisted me in adding the finishing touches. Everything was wrapped magnificently, but there were too many piles to fit under the tree, so we neatly stacked them in front of the fireplace.

Bobby and I started a new tradition with our children, encouraging them to purchase gifts for one another. We gave them each ten dollars and took them to the dollar store to buy a stocking stuffer for everyone. They had a great time shopping for each other and even more fun wrapping and hiding them and presenting them on Christmas day. That idea turned out to be a lifesaver for our first Christmas together.

We woke up Christmas morning, lit the fireplace, fixed a light breakfast, and had family prayer. We decided to open the gifts by age beginning with the youngest. Next, we opened the stocking stuffers. This part of the gift exchange was fun. The kids laughed and were excited about what they had picked out for one another and about what they received.

As our children grew older, we decided to host a Christmas brunch to get everyone together to celebrate and exchange gifts. This schedule keeps us from interfering with the plans of the bio-parents. We start out with prayer, enjoy the creative meal that Bobby and I have planned, open gifts, and then everyone has time to make the other visits that they need to make on Christmas Day. My son Aaron is no longer local, so I miss him terribly during the holidays. However, he makes a visit sometime around my birthday to make up for not being able to be here.

Wedding Anniversaries

Bobby and I married on New Year's Day and always celebrate our anniversary in a grand way by taking a honeymoon trip, usually the first week of the year. We made a promise to each other to always celebrate our anniversary by taking a getaway trip. Based on how close New Year's Day is to the first Sunday, we plan our trip accordingly. We are always excited to make it another year. We love celebrating our anniversary so much that we also celebrate the first day of every month by telling each other happy first!

Many people remember that New Year's is our anniversary and wish us well at watch night service on New Year's Eve. Over the years, our children have rarely acknowledged and never celebrated our anniversary. Perhaps celebrating our wedding anniversary may have been too painful for them. To be excited about our marriage perhaps is a conflict of interest for them. I have concluded that in step-families it is best to just enjoy one another and not force the kids to celebrate. Don't take it personally when your children do not embrace your anniversary. Remember, it is the day that you selected to marry. Make the best of it by planning something extraordinary for the two of you. When you make it special, the children will soon realize how important your anniversary is to you and at least respect your exclusive day.

Once again, living-in-step means finding your own way to celebrate holidays and annual events. Yes, they can be very stressful, but once you establish your own traditions, children will know what to expect. They may still desire things the way they used to be, but the sooner you establish new traditions, the better for everyone. Try to work with the bio-parents to coordinate birthday celebrations and other events involving the children as much as possible. Another point to remember is children like waking up in whatever they call home on Christmas mornings. Again, work with the bio-parent. You cannot only save money by purchasing joint gifts and splitting the costs, but you can also show the child you can work with the other parent on their behalf. However, if the bio-parent is not willing to work with you, find a way to make holidays and other unique occasions, special in your home.

Stepmom Survival Tips

1. Acknowledge and respect old holiday traditions, but establish new ones for your stepfamily.
2. Keep a family calendar and record all events at the beginning of the year. Share dates with everyone involved.
3. Discuss and plan ahead for annual events.
4. Discuss and coordinate gift buying with the bio-parent when possible. Avoid competing for children's affections by trying to outdo the other parent.
5. The bio-parent should assist children in celebrating for the other bio-parent. The stepparent can assist where needed.
6. Acknowledge any efforts made by your stepchildren to include you in holidays/annual events.
7. Suggest to the children they acknowledge the stepparent on special events, but do not force them to participate. Model appropriate behavior.
8. Birthday parties and such should be held in a neutral location, with both bio-parents sharing expenses.
9. Remember Mother's Day and Father's Day should be special for the biological parent.
10. Don't take it personally when your kids don't celebrate or acknowledge your wedding anniversary.

Helpful Scriptures

Exodus 20:12 (KJV)
Honour thy father and thy mother: that thy days may be long upon the land which the LORD thy God giveth thee.

Genesis 40:20-22 (NIV)
Now the third day was Pharaoh's birthday, and he gave a feast for all his officials. He lifted up the heads of the chief cupbearer and the chief baker in the presence of his officials:

Exodus 25:2 (KJV)
Speak unto the children of Israel, that they bring me an offering: of every man that giveth it willingly with his heart ye shall take my offering.

Acts 20:35 (KJV)
I have shewed you all things, how that so labouring ye ought to support the weak, and to remember the words of the Lord Jesus, how he said, It is more blessed to give than to receive.

Colossians 2:16 (NIV)
Therefore do not let anyone judge you by what you eat or drink, or with regard to a religious festival, a New Moon celebration or a Sabbath day. These are a shadow of the things that were to come; the reality, however, is found in Christ.

Chapter Seven

Can We All Just Get Along?

Then our sons in their youth will be like well-nurtured plants, and our daughters will be like pillars carved to adorn a palace. Psalm 144:12 (NIV)

A United Front

When my first husband and I divorced, we made a pact to be supportive of our children and to be cordial in their presence as well as in public venues. We agreed to put our own feelings aside and show solidarity as much as possible. As the custodial parent, I kept the bio-dad informed of events, such as games, school plays, parent teacher conferences, and other school and church related events our children were involved in. Because we were both extremely busy, we often compared schedules to make sure at least one of us could attend or support the majority of their activities. If we both attended, we sat together. When Bobby and I got married, this behavior continued, all three of us sat together with Bobby in the middle holding a conversation with me and the bio-dad. When the bio-dad remarried, there were four of us present and united in support of our children.

Although our intentions were good, when it came to supporting Bobby's kids, we were never quite as successful. In the very beginning of our marriage, it was difficult for Bobby and the bio-mom to be in each other's presence. Being a pastor, Bobby was well known in the community as a leader and also as a parent. Because there were six children in their household, they were popular parents, and we were always running into someone who knew him because of their children. After we married, not everyone knew he had gone through a divorce and had remarried, so sometimes our family matters became the topic of discussion amongst the parents. We observed the whispering and pointing, which was especially uncomfortable for Bobby. I didn't know a lot of people in the neighborhood, so I was not bothered as much by the gossip. All of Bobby's children were very active in school activities, including sports, band, drill team, and other activities. They had also been taught to support each other by attending one another's events. Anytime there was an event, his children could look into the audience and see at least five or more people (sometimes up to twenty) cheering them on. If more than one child had an event, Bobby and the bio-mom worked together to make sure someone attended. The bio-mom's family was supportive and attended many of his children's events. The crowd was intimidating at first, but I learned to live with it.

I.   Sports and Games

All year round, someone was involved in something: basketball, gymnastics, football, track, drill team, and cheerleading. Getting married in January put us right in the middle of basketball season. Among the Love children, Brody was playing college basketball and Jamie was playing girls' basketball in a league at the Salvation Army. My son Aaron was playing high school basketball, and Aiden, my daughter, was enrolled in gymnastics two nights a week. As we discussed getting married, we didn't realize how much time would be spent sitting on wooden or metal benches watching sporting events. The first weekend after we were married, the Love kids were with us. Jamie had a basketball game scheduled for 8:00 AM Saturday morning. We all got up early, loaded up the Cadillac, and went to the

Salvation Army gymnasium to support Jamie. Because Jamie had to be there early, we had our selection of seats to choose from. We selected the top row at the far end of the gym and were six people deep. We were laughing and having a good time watching the girls warm up for the game. I thought to myself, other than having to get up so early this wasn't too bad. As always, I jumped to conclusions too soon.

Right after the game began; the bio-mom came in unaccompanied and sat at the other end of the gymnasium. The boys waved at her, as we all did. Within minutes of the bio-mom's arrival, the attitude of the boys changed dramatically, and they weren't interested in talking to us or looking like they were having fun. Brandon asked if he could go and sit with the bio-mom. I glanced down and saw that she appeared lonely and knew she wasn't accustomed to being by herself. I tried to put myself in her shoes. I sensed it was difficult for her to see all of us together, cheering Jamie on, looking like one happy family. I also supposed the boys were uncomfortable and felt guilty and saddened as if they had abandoned her. We made it through the game, but it was awkward for everyone. After the game ended, I didn't feel it was appropriate for me to get in the middle of the parents' huddle to find out when the next practice was, or hear the feedback on how the girls had played. I stayed to the side and made small talk with my children. The next Saturday would bring another game.

When the next Saturday came, the kids were with the bio-mom, and Bobby and I were alone. This time the bio-mom came with a full posse, and Bobby and I sat at the opposite end of the gym. The kids did not cross the barrier to come over to sit with us, but they waved from a distance. After the game, the bio-mom wanted to have a private conversation with me. This was the first time we had spoken in five months and there were several things she wanted to discuss with me. Because it was the first time any of our children had seen us talking to each other, I didn't want to make the situation any more uncomfortable than it already was. I knew it was not the time or the place to engage in a confrontational conversation, but I could not manage to ignore her request. The kids, her family, and Bobby watched nervously from a distance hoping there would not be a scene. I let the bio-mom ask a round of questions about Bobby and me and my interactions with her children. She also cautioned me not to question her children about anything. Not wanting to be argumentative, I kindly informed her we all needed to work together as much as possible. The dialogue appeared to be moving towards contention, so I suggested we speak at another time and walked away. Bobby and I decided it might be best if we not place ourselves in those circumstances again, at least for a while. For the next year, we made a very conscious decision to sit opposite the bio-mom in separate sections of the gym, stadium, or auditorium.

When Bobby and I married, Aaron was on the sophomore basketball team and also played junior varsity. His games usually occurred in the middle of the week, right after school. In order for me to attend his games, I had to leave work early. Sometimes Bobby would join me. We decided not to pressure each other to attend kid events if we had something important to do. When Aaron made the varsity team, Bobby and I attended Friday and Saturday games together.

Football season was the busiest. Bobby's youngest son Brandon had waited all of his life to play football and had joined a little league team playing mostly on Saturdays. My son Aaron had never played football and was not much of a fan, so I couldn't remember the last time I had attended a football game. In fact, I had never been to a little league game. My daughter Aiden had never been to a football game. When Brandon started playing, we tried to be supportive by attending all of his games. Fortunately, they were on Saturdays. When the kids were at our house, we all went until it got really cold, and then I gave Aiden the choice of whether or not she wanted to attend.

All of our children lived in the same school district, but attended different feeder schools. I was deliberate about not wanting our kids to attend the same schools. It was confusing to the school staff when Bobby was listed as a parent on registration forms for my children and when I was listed on his kids' forms. When I listed Bobby as a guardian on my daughter's forms, the school office staff accidentally printed her name in the directory with the bio-mom's address and phone number. Aiden came home with the directory, upset about the way it was printed. It took several calls to the school to fix the error. I can't imagine what else could have happened if they attended the same schools.

II.   School Events (Plays, Teachers Conferences, Graduations, Field Trips)

Having school age children meant there was always something that needed a parent's presence. Parent teacher conferences came twice a year along with plays and concerts. We considered these events low on the radar screen, so we did not always make an effort to attend these events as a family. My children did not seemed bothered if Bobby didn't attend their activities, but Bobby's kids sometimes asked why I hadn't attended theirs. They were used to having a lot of people at their events and it was their expectation that I should be there as well. Bobby explained I had to work or had something going on with one of my kids.

Graduation is another story because it is an important event in a child's life. So far, we have had four graduations from college and three high school graduations. When possible, we tried to present a united front, particularly because of limited seating. In our town, graduating seniors are given only six tickets per graduate. Once the bio-mom remarried, we had to scrounge to get enough graduation tickets for all of the parents, stepparents, and grandparents to attend graduation ceremonies. We were blessed, and somehow the problem worked itself out, and we all sat together.

Along with graduation, there was customarily a graduation party within the same month. When my son Aaron graduated high school, Bobby and I hosted a small graduation party. The bio-dad attended as a guest and blended well in the crowd. When Brody graduated from college, the bio-mom hosted a graduation get together at his apartment immediately after commencement, but we were not invited. We celebrated by attending the ceremony and giving him a gift. We planned ahead for Brayden's graduation from high school by co-hosting an open house celebration in a neutral location. Bobby rented the party room, and the bio-mom provided the food and the decorations. When Jamie finished high school, we managed to have a joint party for her as well. By the time my daughter graduated from high school, her father was remarried and we co-hosted her graduation party at our house and shared the costs. We have one more high school graduation to go. Hallelujah!

III. Church Events
Church events sometimes presented a unique challenge for our stepfamily. Our children attended church with us on our weekends and with the other bio-parent on their weekends. All of our children were mostly involved in activities at our church because we all resided in Olathe. Both of the other churches they attended were at least twenty miles away. Whenever the kids participated in Easter or Christmas plays, we didn't have to worry about either of the bio-parents wanting to attend.

When Aiden accepted Christ, we were faced with a dilemma. Because the bio-dad was a pastor, he wanted to baptize her at his church. There was not going to be a baptism without me being there, so we discussed how we could make it happen to her satisfaction. We agreed on a baptism date. Being in attendance was going to be difficult for me and Bobby, but because it was such an important event, we would make it work. Bobby and I attended our First Sunday meeting and part of Sunday School, and then left our church and drove twenty miles across town to attend Aiden's baptism at her father's church. The bio-dad was very cordial by allowing me to assist in getting Aiden dressed and preparing her. Bobby was allowed to participate also in the baptism. Prior to the baptism, the bio-dad introduced us to his congregation and Bobby was asked to do a prayer. Everything worked out great, and it was a blessed event for all of us, especially Aiden. Putting aside our differences and focusing on the child made all the difference in the world.

IV.   Miscellaneous

My daughter Aiden had the misfortune to develop appendicitis resulting in an appendectomy. The night she went in the hospital, we made a call to the bio-dad and then drove to the emergency room. The bio-dad and his wife met Bobby and me at the hospital. Once Aiden was checked in, the bio-dad accompanied me to the room with her. Bobby and Aiden's stepmom remained in the lobby for at least three hours. Throughout the entire ordeal, the four of us worked together for the sake of Aiden to make sure she had everything she needed. Once she went home, we allowed the bio-dad and wife to visit her in her bedroom. Once again, our differences had to be put aside for the sake of our child. I wasn't real excited about having the bio-dad and his wife in our private living space, but because of what Aiden had been through, she needed the support and love of all four of us. Aiden's stepmom even brought groceries by while Aiden was recovering. I was very appreciative of their assistance and support.

Bobby's children experienced a number of doctor's visits or surgeries in which we had to support them from a distance. We were able to attend and spend time in the waiting room, but did not have the option to visit with them after they went home. It was especially difficult for Bobby because he wanted to be by their bedside to express his love and concern, and physically care for them. The availability of Bobby's parents served as an opportunity for Bobby and the bio-mom to work together when his children were too sick to go to school. Grandma Love allowed the children to stay at their home where both Bobby and the bio-mom could check on them during the day. We are grateful for Bobby's parents who provided a safe place for all our children.

I can't express enough how important it is for the adults to be mature and work with the bio-parents for the sake of your children. I know it can be tough because you divorced for a reason; however, when the parents try to cooperate with one another, living-in-step can be much easier. As the biological parent, set the example by working with the other parent. Regardless of what has happened in the past, make a pact with the bio-parent to do whatever it takes to support your children. Encourage your spouse to do the same. It will make your interactions with the bio-parent less strenuous, and the children will not be on edge when everyone is in the same space. In fact, children of divorced parents fare better if their parents work together for the sake of their children. Cooperation and working together does not mean that you have to be their best friend. You don't have to like them to work with them; just remember how much you love your child.

Following my daughter Aiden's high school graduation, she personally thanked me for working with the bio-dad and for making what could be a difficult situation more comfortable for her friends and her. I tried to blow her comments off as minor, but she said, "No, Mom, really, you don't understand. I really appreciate it." She shared that her teachers and friends often complimented us on our ability to work together. Some of her friends' parents were divorced and could not tolerate being in the same room together. Her friends had shared that they wished their divorced parents could get along like the bio-dad and I did. I was surprised by her comments and shared that we did it just for her. I promised her we would continue to present a united front to support her in all phases of her life.

Finally, as a stepparent, understand your role. Again there are no ex-parents, only ex-spouses. Never try to outdo the bio-parent by being super stepmom. Nobody can parent your children as well as you can, so don't try to prove you are a better mother to your stepchildren than the bio-mom is. Nothing will start an argument quicker than you trying to tell other people how to raise their children. Be determined and conscientious not to bad mouth biological parents and encourage your spouse to do the same. Remember, the child is part of both parents and often possesses many of their personality traits good or bad. If you bad mouth their parent, in essence, you are badmouthing the child. Such behavior can have an emotional impact on the child. Furthermore, do not allow children to bad mouth the parent or stepparent. Be aware when children try to pit one parent against another to get their way. Learn to be congenial with the bio-parent as much as possible. As a general rule, be a support and always take the high road. Live by the golden rule..."Do unto others as you would have them do unto you." Do it for the children's sake.

Stepmom Survival Tips

1. Keep the bio-parent informed of all children's activities. Make copies of important papers and schedules.
2. Support children as a united front with the bio-parents as much as possible.
3. Discuss with your children that you will do your best to attend their events, but may not make them all.
4. Never make a scene at children's events or do anything that will embarrass you and your spouse or your children.
5. Encourage the children to thank the stepparent for attending their activities.
6. As a stepparent, participate as a silent supportive partner. Don't give unsolicited advice.
7. Plan graduation celebrations and other special celebrations with the bio-parent.
8. Plan ahead for events in which parental information must be printed. Make sure everyone's name is included.
9. Consult with your spouse to identify those events that you would really appreciate his or presence. Use a rating system.
10. Do not compete with the bio-parent; be motivated by love for the child.

Helpful Scriptures

Proverbs 23:24-25 (NIV)
The father of a righteous man has great joy; he who has a wise son delights in him. May your father and mother be glad; may she who gave you birth rejoice!

Proverbs 27:11 (NKJV)
My son, be wise, and make my heart glad, That I may answer him who reproaches me.

1 Samuel 2:26 (NKJV)
And the child Samuel grew in stature, and in favor both with the LORD and men.

Deuteronomy 6:7 (KJV)
And thou shalt teach them diligently unto thy children, and shalt talk of them when thou sittest in thine house, and when thou walkest by the way, and when thou liest down, and when thou risest up.

Proverbs 3:1 (NIV)
My son, do not forget my teaching, but keep my commands in your heart, for they will prolong your life many years and bring you prosperity.

Chapter Eight

Love and Money

If you love money and wealth, you will never be satisfied with what you have. This doesn't make sense either. Ecclesiastes 5:10 (CEV)

As a Christian counselor, when Bobby provides premarital counseling, he will most always give the couple a temperament assessment and then expend much energy helping them to understand not only themselves, but their mates' dispositions. Part of helping them to understand their makeup involves open discussion of their views and beliefs about money, and encouraging them to have open, honest, conversations about how they plan to manage their finances. Disagreements about money have been cited as one of the major reasons first-time couples divorcing. Living-in-step only complicates financial matters. If minor children are involved, most likely your spouse is paying child support and perhaps alimony. You may be receiving money from the bio-dad. As a stepfamily, its best to discuss these matters before marriage and lay them all out on the table.

How Did My Mom Do It?

I grew up in a very traditional home where my dad worked a full-time job to support our family, and my mom stayed home during our elementary years. Dad was fortunate to be an employee of the United State Postal Service, which was a dependable job with great benefits. He was also a veteran and received additional income because of a war injury. My mother worked part-time when we were younger then accepted a position as the director of our church day care center. Between the two of them, they probably earned less than $30,000 a year.

Twice a month when my dad received his payroll check, he gave Mom what he thought was enough money to run the household. She had to pay bills, buy groceries, and pay for our school lunches and any other items the four of us needed. The amount he gave her did not change even as we got older. Once in a while, when we needed something requiring additional money, Mom secretly complained to us that Dad should start giving her more money. Dad controlled the rest of the money, and Mom didn't ask a whole lot of questions. He thought what he gave her was plenty, but it was also his way of controlling how much she had available to give to the church. Somehow, Mom managed to create a certain standard of living for us, and at the same time taught us the principles of giving and tithing.

In reality, Mom often did without and rarely bought anything for herself. She got new clothes only when Christmas or Mother's Day came around. Watching my mom struggle and often do without was difficult for me. I admire Mom for how she cared for us girls, but I was often angered by her level of submission to my dad. In my mind, she was too dependent on him for money. As I began to think about my future as a wife and a mother, I resolved never to depend on a man to take care of me, nor allow him to control the money. I would go to college, get a good job, and take care of myself. No one, not even my husband was going to tell me how to spend my money, particularly if I wanted to give to the church.

Learning to be Content

After finishing four years of college, I continued on to graduate school. Once my master's degree was completed, I immediately went to work full time and have worked consistently ever since. Much of my career has been in management, and I have been blessed and most fortunate to have wonderful and fulfilling jobs. Opportunities and promotions came regularly, and God granted favor by providing what I needed to be successful even in jobs I didn't feel I was qualified for.

After relocating from Oklahoma to Kansas City with my first husband, I didn't go to work immediately. The organization I worked with in Oklahoma City was closing operations; therefore, I was provided a generous severance. I was also eligible for unemployment. The move was stressful for the kids, so I chose to focus on getting them settled and let my ex-husband focus on the job that had relocated us, and his new position as a pastor. After five months of being at home and craving adult conversations, I began to search for a job. Salary offers came at a much lower rate than I had been paid previously. Money wasn't the motivating factor as much as wanting to be in a health care environment, so I accepted a position that offered the most potential for advancement and growth.

About six months before our divorce, my ex-husband left his vice-president position to become a full time pastor. Our annual incomes were roughly the same; therefore, when our divorce financial documents were calculated, we were responsible for the same amount of financial support for our kids. In other words, I wasn't getting a whole lot of child support. Following the divorce, it was important to me to support my family in the manner we were accustomed to. Fortunately, when we sold our house, we made a huge profit that helped us to transition into our separate lives.

It didn't take long to find a higher paying job. The increase in salary allowed me the opportunity to purchase a house, so we could get out of the townhouse. There was enough money to travel and afford the simple things we enjoyed, like eating out and shopping. It is no secret that I enjoy shopping and buying shoes on sale; however, I had my priorities in order and always paid tithes and offerings to the church. Bills were paid on time, and money was stored in savings for my children's education and retirement accounts. The Lord also blessed me with consultant work reviewing grants when I needed additional money. God is always true to His promise to open up windows and pour me out blessings, just when I need them.

Money and Marriage

When Bobby and I married, I owned a four bedroom home, a late model car, and had a positive financial portfolio. Bobby's finances weren't so positive. It is not difficult to figure out that in today's society, kids cost money and Bobby had six. He supported his family by working for the city and being a full-time pastor. Both of Bobby's salaries were used to pay child support and alimony in addition to several car payments, automobile insurance, and college tuition. As long as he had two jobs, our finances were manageable because there was some money that remained in our household, although it wasn't much. In the beginning, it really didn't bother me that most of his money went to another household. I knew all too well what divorce can do to a family's financial situation. With so much money going to the bio-mom's house, I hoped and prayed that there would be less friction between them.

Because I didn't want to stretch Bobby's money any further, it was decided, by default, that I continue to cover the household expenses, including the house payment and utilities. Bobby was responsible for the car insurance, which included up to five cars. Yes, our automobile insurance was almost as much as our house payment. This bill paying arrangement kept the negotiations to a minimum; in fact, we rarely had to discuss money.

A few weeks before our wedding, we opened separate checking and savings accounts and granted access to one another's account.

One of the reasons we chose to keep our accounts separate was our different ways of managing our financial records. Regularly balancing my account, I knew exactly how much was available at any given time. I was very deliberate in spending and often planned for big purchases. All bills were paid on time and saving was included in the budget.

Bobby, on the other hand, balanced his checkbook only when there was a problem and used the internet or telephone banking to make sure checks cleared his account. Bills were paid when the money was available or once a month, whichever came first, regardless of when they were due, however, the child support and alimony were paid on time. Bobby also rarely opened bills because he knew what was owed. On a couple of occasions there was a check in the envelope instead of a bill, and it would have been missed had I not been going through mail to shred old bills.

Even though we handled our accounts and bills differently, we had some areas in common. Tithing was important, as well as charitable giving. We both had an appreciation for finer things within our budget. If our parents were in need, we didn't hesitate to help them. Money was spent on children, and they had what they needed and some of their wants, within limits. My kids often complained that I refused to buy the things that many of their friends had such as expensive video games and expensive tennis shoes. They said I bought them what they needed and their father bought them what they wanted. "Great!" I often replied, "I'm not going to ruin you by buying you everything you want."

Financial Changes

After we married, Bobby's ministry at the church was strained. There was turmoil in the church because some members were unhappy with his life choices and were very vocal about it. Working a full-time job, it became increasingly difficult for him to dedicate the time needed to help the church heal emotionally. His parents were aging, and they were dependent on him for assistance in several areas such as transportation to doctor's appointments, sorting out medications, financial matters, and other important business. Being a newlywed and adjusting to our marriage also required time and energy. There weren't enough hours in a day, and all of the juggling was causing a considerable amount of stress on him. We were happy, but I could tell Bobby was struggling as he attempted to help everyone including himself.

One day I was at work and received a phone call from Bobby. He hesitated before he spoke and really didn't sound like himself. He called to inform me he was sitting in the parking lot of the Olathe hospital and was about to go into the emergency room because of chest pains. He was afraid that he was having a heart attack. I left work immediately and thought to myself, "This man is killing himself." I prayed real hard, "Please God, don't take him away from me." We were grateful that it turned out to be an anxiety attack.

After the emergency room visit, we began praying and analyzing our financial situation. Although we wanted to buy another house, we decided we didn't want to increase our expenses right away; therefore, about eight months after we married, Bobby left his full-time job with the city. This decision was based on the need to focus more on the church and his parents, children, and our marriage.

Although this decision significantly reduced Bobby's stress level, our household income decreased by a minimum of one third. The city job had provided health care coverage for Bobby and his children. Working at a health care organization, I was blessed to be able to carry everyone on my health insurance. Now that we had the same expenses with less money, we began to have a few more conversations regarding financial matters. Being faithful tithers, we held fast to God's word that he would bless our decision. Slowly, the Lord began to replace Bobby's income by increasing mine. Please allow me to share my story because it may encourage someone to keep on tithing and giving to the Lord, despite circumstances.

Not long after Bobby left the city job, my sister called me and was in need of $500. Things were tight for us, but there was money in our savings account. I discussed it with Bobby, and we sent her the money, praying no emergencies would come our way. A week later, a check came in the mail from my dentist, indicating an overpaid dental bill. The check totaled fifty-five dollars. I counted it a blessing for helping my sister out.

Bobby loved to cook and often prepared scrumptious meals, which became a real challenge to maintain my weight. My friend and hairdresser, Luttra, convinced me to join her Jazzercise group. To boost their enrollment numbers, they frequently offered contests and raffles for bringing a friend who joined also. Our class started at 5:30 AM, and it was best to have a friend to hold you accountable to get up and go to class Monday thru Friday. I finally convinced my friend Tina to join me. One sleepy morning after arriving to class, the check-in attendant informed me that she had a surprise for me. My name had been placed in a drawing for bringing a friend that joined. I was the lucky winner and won $500. My sister also sent her $500 to repay the loan. I was now $555 dollars ahead. What a blessing.

Several calls began to come in offering consultant work. I was paid $250 to participate in conference calls or $1000-$2000 to review grants. In May of 2004, I was fortunate to receive a promotion on my job. Once I moved to my new job, my employer was unable to find a replacement, so I was asked to do both jobs temporarily. A generous $5,000 bonus was given for working both jobs. Do you get the picture? The Lord kept blessing, so we hardly missed the income Bobby had made with the City. Bobby stayed on top of his child support and the other bills he was responsible for. We used his annual bonus around appreciation time to cover our annual anniversary trip and extra expenses that we incurred during the year. In fact, the first year he left his full time job, we traveled more than we ever had.

The Guilt Trip

I perceived that it bothered Bobby for his children to live in much different circumstances than what he provided for them as a live-in father. Although he paid a substantial amount of money in child support and alimony, it wasn't enough for the bio-mom to maintain her former standard of living. The children often asked for clothes and money, and sporadically mentioned they were hungry when they got home from school. After Bobby left the city, he made arrangements to pick the kids up from school every day. Once he picked them up, he took them to our house and prepared a small meal for them. The meal wasn't just an afternoon snack, but a mini dinner meal. I thought he might be ruining their dinner by feeding them so much. He explained he felt better if he could see their feet under our table and knew they were fed before they went home to the bio-mom's house. Feeding them helped him to connect with his children and indirectly helped the bio-mom out.

Bobby, like his mother (Mother Love), shows his love by feeding and caring for others. He wanted his children to know regardless of life's circumstances, they could always come to our house for a hot meal. He valued the time spent with them, thereby giving him an opportunity to monitor their study habits and assist with homework. I applauded his efforts and appreciated having dinner on the table when I arrived home from work. After doing the cooking for a full semester, he began to complain of feeling too domesticated. Bobby found himself spending more time in the kitchen cooking and cleaning, and did not like his new role. I didn't mind cooking dinner; it just seemed to be more convenient for him because he was already in the kitchen, cooking a meal for his children. When I came home from work and the house smelled of food, I thought dinner was already prepared and eagerly inquired, "What's for dinner?"

I understood his frustration and inquired as to why he felt the need to prepare such a large meal every day after school. I soon discovered much of his behavior was related to the guilt he experienced not being a custodial parent. He did not like the disparity in living arrangements and tried to compensate as best he could. It was tough for him not to care for them on a daily basis. I encouraged him to be creative and not wear himself out in the process. He continued to pick the kids up from school as his schedule permitted.

College Tuition

The time came for my son Aaron to go to college. He chose a university in North Carolina and was awarded a few small scholarships to cover books; but tuition, room and board, and other expenses were not covered. The bio-dad and I worked out an arrangement to split the expenses, and thankfully, we had enough to cover his expenses for the first two years. At enrollment time, Bobby assured me that whatever I had to do, he supported it. I thanked him for his support, but silently knew that regardless, paying for college expenses was still my responsibility. By this stage, we were no longer paying tuition for Bobby's daughter because she began receiving additional financial aid. Everything was working out fine.

The Lord continued to bless us through my job, and I received another promotion. The new position included a raise to help out with tuition payments, and it helped to take the pressure off of us financially. We still had money in the bank and some money in the savings account. As indicated in the chapter entitled "Trading Spaces," we finally decided to buy a house together. The new payment doubled, almost tripled, the current house payment.

No More Expenses Please!

Our first major disagreement about money occurred when Bobby's daughter's Janae needed to have her car replaced. Because her car was paid off, buying another one meant adding another car payment to our budget. Overall, we were doing okay financially, but an additional $150-200 to our budget was not something that I wanted to do at the time. In my opinion, a car for a college student was a luxury, not a necessity so it could wait. Bobby acknowledged that per the divorce agreement, he was responsible for paying for cars while his children attended college. He agreed with me in the short run, but soon decided to purchase another car on his own.

We were fortunate to have a deacon in our church who was a car dealer and who assisted Bobby with most of his car purchases. They found a car and worked out a payment for $150.00 a month. The car was titled in Janae and Bobby's names, and it was agreed that she would cover the payments during the summer months while working a summer job. I wasn't happy with his decision, but decided to keep my mouth shut to maintain peace. However, in my mind, I dared him to complain later when we needed additional money to cover unexpected expenses.

What About Me?

I cannot stress enough the importance of complete disclosure about finances before you marry. Not only should you disclose your current financial situation, but also discuss money management. Do not assume money matters will just work out. Do yourself a favor and take the guesswork out. So far in this chapter, it appears as though we rarely experienced money struggles. Early in our marriage, discussing money appeared to be somewhat of a taboo. I already knew Bobby's situation, having to pay child support, alimony, and other bills. With so much going to the other household, he would have needed another job to assist with expenses in our household.

After we married, I continued to cover all of the bills as I did as the head of household, given the mortgage and utilities were in my name. "No worries," I thought, "I am no worse off than I was." I was thankful my income was more than enough to cover everything without straining. At least, I no longer had to cover my car insurance. An added bonus was Bobby did most of the grocery shopping. We didn't have excess, but we were okay. Besides, me paying most of the bills wasn't permanent. I kept reminding myself of the future when Bobby would no longer have to pay alimony or child support. The excitement of future days managed to keep me focused and positive most of the time.

However, there were times when Satan entered my spirit, and I became annoyed, maybe even angry, particularly when a request came for additional money. It wasn't so bad when Bobby worked at the city, but once he received only the church income, he didn't have much left over. In special circumstances, I became the backup plan. Brody and Janae were in college and occasionally needed assistance. When Brody needed money for books, without hesitation, I wrote a check from my account and sent it. On one occasion Janae didn't have enough money to cover her monthly apartment expenses. She telephoned Bobby in fear of a utility being disconnected. Bobby explained his limitations, and suggested a call to me, since the bio-mom could not assist either. In desperation, I was called. During our discussion, I explained to Janae that I felt used because our relationship was not all that great, yet she was asking me for money. I did, however, go ahead and help out, but I was not happy about additional spending.

In an attempt to explain my feelings to Bobby, I labeled my association with his children, "a relationship of convenience." The only time I heard from his older children was when they needed something and discovered I was the gatekeeper or their only option. I'm sure his children felt grateful, but I very seldom received thanks. I really felt like I was being taken advantage of.

Once we moved into our new home, after paying bills, buying additional furniture, and paying two house payments because the other house had not yet sold, the balance in my checking account was $100. I managed to move money around between accounts to get us through the month. I was frightened, and praying that the other house would sell soon. The more frightened I was, the more frustrated I became. I didn't know whether to be angry at Bobby or at the bio-mom. Why did they decide to have so many kids? Didn't they know it takes a lot of money to raise that many kids? I wanted my husband to be able to spend money on me and buy me something extravagant like an expensive coat or something, rather than paying for everyone else. I didn't even expect much in the form of gifts, but longed for the time when Bobby wasn't supporting another household.

Career Women

The Stepfamily Foundation reports most women who marry men with children are career women, meaning they are employed, self-sustained and have their own money. The more I thought about this, I was more and more grateful that I did not enter the marriage dependent on my husband for financial resources. I can't imagine what our lives would have been like if I didn't have a career. Once again, I strongly suggest having serious discussions about finances and laying everything out on the table before marrying. Please do not go into a marriage blindly.

Divorce places a huge financial strain on both parties, and nobody comes out whole. Non-custodial parents often feel like they do not have enough money to have a decent quality of life, after child support/alimony is paid. Case in point, Bobby stayed with his parents following his divorce because he paid out so much. If he would have secured an apartment, meeting his monthly obligations would have been a struggle for him. On the other hand, the custodial parents argue more money is needed to take care of the children than what is provided monthly. Once I found out how much Bobby was paying in child support and alimony, I felt like I had been short changed all the way around. However, I trusted God to provide for me, and I had compassion on the bio-mom who was struggling financially to support her home.

Living-in-step means that money can become even more complicated. It is highly possible that money is being exchanged across several households. In our case, we knew of money being exchanged between at least four households. For instance, after Bobby and I married, eventually both of our ex-spouses remarried. I was receiving child support from the bio-dad, and Bobby was paying child support and alimony to the bio-mom. The bio-mom's new spouse was providing support for his children who lived out of state. The bio-dad's wife was receiving support for her daughter. Believe me, it's complicated when it comes to paying and receiving child support and/or alimony. It is only after children are grown that money stops being exchanged as mandated by law.

Be aware that different states have different regulations regarding child support. In the state of Kansas, child support ends once a child is eighteen and graduates from high school. Speaking with friends who live in other states, child support continues while the child attends college. In addition, there could be alimony paid to the ex-spouse. Alimony has its own set of rules and timelines. I can't even remember how long Bobby paid alimony. Asking questions would have frustrated both of us, so I didn't ask why he signed up to pay so many years of alimony. His divorce arrangement was complete and in process prior to my coming on the scene. I accepted them at face value and would suggest you do the same.

Emotions come and go with the monthly exchange of money. When the remarried, non-custodial, bio-dad takes on the responsibility of a new wife, he can feel pulled in different directions. His new wife may have desires and needs that may be neglected because there is little money left. The children may be angry because they have less, and it appears that Dad's new household has more. They may even compare and complain openly. The bio-mom may decide to return to court to get additional money when she feels like she and her children are being slighted. It happens. If she does return to court, keep in mind that your income is now included in the calculation of the household income.

Biblical Financial Study

In year seven of our marriage, we participated in a biblical financial study produced by Crown Financial Ministries. We also introduced this study to a group of members in our church family. While participating in the Crown class, Bobby and I were much more willing to discuss our finances. For a long time, we had separate money, accounts, bills, and plans. We now work together on our financial dreams and goals and pray for God's guidance on how we manage our finances. God has continued to bless us despite our expenses. We are grateful that God provides for us so abundantly.

Any marriage has the potential to have conflicts over the distribution of money. You don't have to be living-in-step to fight about money; therefore, I encourage couples to participate in a biblical financial study together. I am partial to Crown Ministries because it has been such a blessing to Bobby and me and our church family. Learn what God has to say about how you manage the other ninety percent of your finances. Of course, we know that ten percent belongs to him. II Chronicles 29:11-12 (TLB) reads, "Everything in the heavens and earth is yours, O Lord, and this is your kingdom. We adore you as being in control of everything. Riches and honor come from you alone and you are the ruler of all mankind. Your hand controls power and might and it is at your discretion that men are made great and given strength."

As a result of this study, I have come to realize that God is the supplier of my needs, not my job or my husband. Trusting God to provide for us gives me peace not to worry about how much is going out or coming in, because ultimately, as written in Philippians 4:29, I know "God will supply all my needs according to his riches in glory." I no longer get angry or fretful, when we have unexpected or planned costs for our children. Having this peace can do wonders for your marriage.

Stepmom Survival Tips

1. Understand finances can be more complicated when living-in-step.
2. Discuss money and financial management before you get married. Review incoming and outgoing expenses, divorce decrees, and other important financial documents.
3. Make sure your spouse is responsible and pays child support/alimony regularly and on time.
4. Be willing to help out where you can, even if you don't feel appreciated. Pray about feelings of anger and frustration.
5. Pray about attitudes of my money/your money. Pray for a position of "our money." Where possible, combine finances and work from joint accounts.
6. Openly discuss additional expenses needed for children.
7. Don't secretly give your children considerable amounts of money or make other crucial financial decisions without discussing with your spouse.
8. Understanding feelings of guilt experienced by non-custodial fathers, but don't openly label him as guilty and being manipulated by his children.
9. Plan for and discuss major expenses like tuition, cars and other big ticket items.
10. Participate in a Biblical financial study class, such as Crown or Dave Ramsey.

Helpful Scriptures

Philippians 4:12-13 (NIV)

I know what it is to be in need, and I know what it is to have plenty. I have learned the secret of being content in any and every situation, whether well fed or hungry, whether living in plenty or in want. I can do all this through him who gives me strength.

Deuteronomy 15:6 (NKJV)

For the LORD your God will bless you just as He promised you; you shall lend to many nations, but you shall not borrow; you shall reign over many nations, but they shall not reign over you.

Acts 20:35b (NIV)

Remember the words of the Lord Jesus, that He Himself said, 'It is more blessed to give than to receive'.

Matthew 6:1 (CEV)

When you do good deeds, don't try to show off. If you do, you won't get a reward from your Father in heaven.

2 Corinthians 9:6-7 (NKJV)

But this I say: He who sows sparingly will also reap sparingly, and he who sows bountifully will also reap bountifully. So let each one give as he purposes in his heart, not grudgingly or of necessity; for God loves a cheerful giver.

Chapter Nine
Step Parenting Can Make You Sick

Be careful for nothing; but in everything by prayer and supplication with thanksgiving let your requests be made known unto God. And the peace of God, which passeth all understanding, shall keep your hearts and minds through Christ Jesus. Philippians 4:6-7 (KJV)

High Expectations

Our expectations were grand for our marriage and our new stepfamily. During the few months while dating, everything had gone so well. There couldn't possibly be major problems for us because we loved each other, and surely our kids would follow suit and be excited about our marriage. My assumption was I could love Bobby's kids as much I loved my own. After all, prior to our getting married, I had a wonderful relationship with his children and was their favorite Sunday school teacher/youth worker. Bobby loved his children and even though his relationship with them was somewhat strained in the beginning, I was determined to include them in our lives and be one big happy family. Besides, we were willing to do whatever it took to make it work.

Living-in-step presented more challenges than ever imagined, and I became disillusioned. I was disappointed in myself that I did not love his children the same way I loved my own children. I felt like I loved his children, but I was beginning to experience negative emotions related to them. This attitude concerned me because I couldn't imagine feeling this way, and it was totally against my Christian principle to try to live peaceably with everyone. What was going on with me?

We weren't naïve of how others felt about our marriage, but we decided to handle all resistance with love, even if we had to cry on each other's shoulder after taking emotional beatings. So far, God had answered our prayers, and although I felt mistreated and rejected, I had no desire to retaliate or destroy anyone. However, negative thoughts and questions began to dominate my thoughts, such as:

- Despite everything I do for his children, buying things, feeding them, providing a safe, warm environment, letting them visit whenever they wanted to, they do not appreciate me!
- They don't even respect their own father and mother, so I don't stand a chance.
- They only put up with me or tolerate me because they know I am the gatekeeper to get to their dad.
- They are so disrespectful for ignoring me and not abiding by my rules.
- When is Bobby going to do something about them treating me this way?

Something is Wrong

The list went on and on. I was extremely critical of myself as I began to experience dismal thoughts and feelings. As visitation weekends approached, or when Bobby's children called on the telephone, I experienced a range of emotions. The actual visit exacerbated the aggravation. Some weekends, my frustration was at an all-time high. As these emotions began, I prayed frequently and fervently, searching for ways to avoid my feelings and conceal them from Bobby. I read every book available to me related to stepparenting, hoping to find someone who had experienced similar struggles. I soon discovered that I was dealing with ambivalence.

Ambivalence: The coexistence within an individual of positive and negative feelings toward the same person, object, or action, simultaneously drawing him or her in opposite directions. (Dictionary.com)

I researched ambivalence and related experiences and learned it can cause severe emotional stress, which if not addressed can lead to stress related health problems. I ran across an internet article entitled "Your Mixed-Feeling Friends May be Bad for Your Health" (Colino 2005). She commented on a study done by researchers at Brigham Young University and the University of Utah. The researchers discovered that "unpredictable and ambivalent friendships" create stress, raise blood pressure, and can contribute to cardiovascular problems (Holt-Lunstad, et al. 2003). This study was similar to another one that found people have higher blood pressure when they are around people who they have mixed feelings about, even more so than being around people they don't like. Based on the study, one is better off loving or hating the person, than experiencing both emotions regarding them. Reading the article helped me to understand what was going on with me. Feelings of love and dislike (I hope it wasn't hate) were going on within me at the same time regarding Bobby's kids. Like Paul said in Romans 7:21, "When I would do right, evil is always present." I wanted to be loving and positive around my stepchildren, but I was struggling.

Towards the end of year two, our situation went from bad to worse, and I began experiencing extreme anxiety whenever I would see, hear, think about, or even talk about my stepchildren. For instance, while cooking dinner one evening, the phone rang, and the caller ID indicated it was one of Bobby's children. Immediately, my heart began racing, my chest tightened, my breathing became shallow, and I felt like I was going to be sick to my stomach.

As visitation weekends approached, the fretfulness and physiological symptoms began on Thursday, remained through the

weekend, and subsided around Tuesday of the following week. I
became a different person, and Bobby and I began to experience
difficulty communicating about his children. I tried to act like nothing
was wrong and as much as possible tried to avoid the subject. During
our alone weekends, Bobby tried to manage my frustration and gain a
better understanding of what was going on with me. I always
explained how stressful my job was rather than admit what was
going on with me in relation to his children. We were headed for
serious trouble or I was more concerned I was going to have a heart
attack.

I Need Therapy

The last medical exam I received revealed that I was physically
healthy. I tried to be health conscious by working out several times a
week and eating a balanced diet. My extensive training in biological
psychology helped me to understand what effects the mind can have
on the body. My anxiety escalated to the point I had uncontrolled
thoughts of doing physical harm to others. Not that I really believed I
could hurt someone, but I daydreamed about bad things happening.
One day while driving, I envisioned it would feel great to commit
road rage.

Through deductive reasoning, I determined my problem was
psychological. I really needed to talk to someone, but I couldn't
discuss my feelings with just anyone. I could not expose myself to
Bobby, friends, church members, or even family. I imagined there
were persons, including our children, who wanted our marriage to
fail and would have delighted in hearing about our problems. With
Bobby being my pastor, I did not have a pastor to set up a counseling
appointment with. I was not aware of any Christian counselors or
therapists that specialized in stepfamilies.

I engaged in brief conversations with other stepmoms to see how
they were handling their situations. Most of them had worse
situations than mine and used the opportunity to complain to me

about their problems. God sent another stepmom who was a former pastor's wife into my life, who offered much encouragement. Beverly and I shared and offered ourselves as support to one another. We talked about our struggles, but I was afraid to admit the anxiety problems I was having.

I prayed for guidance to find a counselor who could help me and provide complete anonymity. Finally, I decided to contact the employee assistance program (EAP) offered by my employer. Having been enrolled in a master's counseling program at one time and serving as a counselor, I knew the benefits of at least three therapy sessions with a licensed therapist. I called the EAP program and arranged a session with a female therapist in close proximity. I wasn't sure how Bobby felt about my going to counseling, but once I informed him, he was supportive as he could be. He knew how much I was struggling.

I worked with a great counselor for weeks talking about our marriage and my relationship with my stepchildren. Given that I had so many stepchildren and each of their personalities were different, I was given additional counseling sessions. My most difficult affiliation was with Bobby's daughters. Janae had expressed on several occasions that her parents' divorce and our remarriage had ruined her life. In my opinion, his younger daughter Jamie despised me and wanted nothing to do with me. I was convinced that they, with the assistance of the bio-mom, wanted to make our lives as miserable as possible. Working with a therapist, I was able to negate the negative thoughts I was having and slightly reduce my stress level.

Although the counseling was helpful, and I had a better understanding of my family dynamics, I was getting worse physically. My symptoms included heart palpitations, breathing problems, digestive problems, heat intolerance, hand trembling, insomnia, and weight loss. Within thirty minutes of eating anything, diarrhea followed. I was sweating while everyone else in the room was comfortable. Sleep was impossible, including difficulty falling asleep and waking up several times during the night. My size went down almost two dress sizes. My clothes no longer fit, and I had to purchase new outfits for work and church. I even tried to convince myself I was losing weight deliberately. I had been working out faithfully to get in shape, so I didn't mind burning extra calories, but the excessive weight loss was getting ridiculous. I was beginning to look like I was suffering from malnutrition or anorexia. Something was seriously wrong with me.

Doctor, Am I Going Through the Change?

Through rationalization and self-diagnosis, I concluded I was preparing for menopause and needed to consider hormone therapy. Although it seemed to be happening earlier than I thought it should be, many of the symptoms were present. Bobby couldn't help but notice the health changes and was worried sick, so he convinced me to schedule an appointment with my primary care physician. Bobby accompanied me to the visit and assisted in describing my physical complaints. We asked if she could test for menopause because we thought my hormones were imbalanced. My doctor explained that some of the symptoms did not sound like menopause and she wanted to run a full blood work panel. She assured us the blood tests would reveal what was going on in my body, and then we could work together to find solutions to help me feel better. She jotted down my phone number and said she would call me personally to share the results as soon as they returned from the lab.

I stayed glued to the phone the next day, waiting on the call from my doctor. When she finally called, she offered a clear explanation of what was causing my physical condition. The blood tests revealed an overactive thyroid with a possible diagnosis of Graves' disease. The symptoms I was experiencing were classic, minus the bulging eyes. My primary care physician could not treat this condition, but was willing to give me something to help me sleep until I could see a specialist. An endocrinologist had to make the final diagnosis and determine treatment. I searched for endocrinologists, but most of them didn't have an opening for a new patient for up to six months. I finally located one who accepted my insurance plan and locked in an appointment within thirty days.

In the meantime, I read anything I could get my hands on related to thyroid hyperactivity. The only thing I knew about Graves' disease was that it made your eyes bulge out. I was aware of the Olympic track star Gale Devers who suffered from the illness. My eyes didn't bulge out, but my doctor was right; I had all of the classic symptoms. In my reading, I wanted to know what caused this disease. While searching the internet, reading books, and talking to physicians at work, I learned the disease could be hereditary or brought on by extreme stress. No one in my family had an overactive thyroid, but my sister had suffered from an underactive one following a pregnancy.

At my first appointment with the endocrinologist, he took the time to explain the disease, treatment options, and what to expect. Radiology and iodine uptake tests confirmed Graves' disease. It was treatable, thank God, and my treatment choices were medication or chemical removal of the thyroid with radioactive iodine. I chose medication and was given three prescriptions: sleeping pills to help me sleep, a beta blocker to slow my heart down, and a thyroid medication to slow down the production of thyroid hormones. He warned me there would be an adjustment period and that he may have to tweak the medication dosage until we found the right combination.

After being on the medications for a week, I felt like I was walking around in a daze, moving in slow motion, and overmedicated. He reduced the beta blockers, but the decrease in meds didn't produce a noticeable change for the better. Finally, after experiencing two nights of mild hallucinations, which really scared Bobby, we requested I be taken off of the beta blockers and the sleeping pill dosage be lowered. Bobby had then placed my name on our church prayer list, and many church members were praying for me. Eventually, I was only taking the thyroid pills.

Slowly, my health began to improve, and after being on the thyroid regime for four months, most of the prominent symptoms began to disappear. Eight months later, we were able to reduce my medication to half and then down to one pill every other day. The first week of June the following year, my doctor announced I was in remission. I was taken off medication, and we praised God for my healing. All I had to do was to stay in remission for a year, and I would be considered healed. I claimed the healing and constantly prayed the Graves' disease was gone for good. As long as I kept my stress levels low, I could remain in remission. By the way, during my treatment, my mom was diagnosed with Graves' disease and had her thyroid chemically removed.

I'm Sick to My Stomach

Although I was feeling better physically, my relationship with and thoughts about Bobby's kids hadn't necessarily improved. We were in year three, and for the first time since we had been married, the bio-mom was going out of town for almost two weeks. We were happy for her to get away, but her travels meant the kids would be with us the entire time. What was I going to do for ten days? Bobby was energized because it was our first opportunity to have Thanksgiving dinner in our new home with his parents and children. I was worried and felt my body reacting to the perceived pressure. My best bet was to be away from the house as much as possible. It was Thanksgiving week and the kids were out of school from Wednesday through the following Monday. I worked on Tuesday and Wednesday, burying myself in my work.

On Thanksgiving Day, we got up early around 5:30 AM to start dinner preparations. The kids had been up late and weren't disturbed by the noise Bobby and I were making in the kitchen. Most of the Thanksgiving dishes including the turkey were finished cooking, with the exception of the cake. Around 11:00, I awakened my daughter, as I had promised she could assist me in baking my world famous pound cake. It was a tradition in my family to prepare holiday meals wearing my grandmother's aprons. After I convinced Aiden to wear the ceremonial apron, we began. We put the cake in the oven, and I used the hour long baking time to take a shower, change clothes, and relax before dinner.

By one o'clock, the doorbell rang, and we laid out the Thanksgiving spread: turkey, cornbread dressing, oyster dressing, ham, sweet potato casserole, greens, green beans, macaroni and cheese, rolls, pound cake, sweet potato pie, and pecan pies. We said a family prayer and devoured the food. All of the kids ate in the dining area attached to the kitchen, and Bobby and I ate in the formal dining room with Bobby's parents. We made it through dinner, and everyone was happy.

Because we were up so early, I decided it was the perfect time to take a nap after the kitchen was cleaned up. My nap lasted about three hours, and I woke up to find the house still alive with happy kids. I went to the basement to talk with my son Aaron until he went out with his friends. The Kansas City Chiefs football game came on, so Bobby was glued to the television; therefore, I went upstairs, finished the book I had been trying to read for a month and watched one of my favorite movies. Before I knew it, I was asleep again, and Thanksgiving was over.

The Friday after Thanksgiving, I decided to spend the day Christmas shopping. My kids were going to the bio-dad's house, so I could disengage. Bobby would be busy hanging Christmas lights most of the day. I picked up my friend Tina and we spent the day searching for Black Friday sales. After a full day of shopping, we were famished. We were tired of Thanksgiving food and were delighted when her daughter-in-law brought a generous serving of Vietnamese stir fry by Tina's house. I hung out until it was dark outside. By the time I arrived home, everyone was gathered in the kitchen eating leftovers. I retreated to our bedroom and didn't come out again. I kept thinking to myself, if I can make it just two more days . . .

Saturday, I got up early, and made it a point again to be gone all day. I came home around the same time to find the same scenario: everyone was gathered in the kitchen surrounded by food. I could not bring myself to eat, so I went to our bedroom to finish preparing my lesson plans for Sunday. My nerves were at their worst, but I kept thinking, just one more day! Sunday wouldn't be too bad because it was always filled with activities, and we had plenty of leftovers to eat so I didn't have to cook a full meal. I felt bad about my behavior, but I just didn't want to be around them. I was doing my part by letting them stay with us and allowing our house to be party headquarters while the bio-mom was gone.

I was awakened around 3:00 o'clock Sunday morning by enormous pains in my stomach. I got out of the bed quickly before an emergency happened. After being in the bathroom for about an hour, I knew I was in trouble. There was no way I was going to make it to Sunday school or worship service. Now my afternoon plans were ruined, as I intended to go to church, have dinner, go to a movie with my daughter Aiden, and then drop by a friend's house for the rest of the evening. The frequent trips to the bathroom convinced me I wasn't about to go anywhere. I was miserable. Once again, I was convinced my stress level had reduced my resistance, and I had caught a stomach virus. In addition, I was ashamed of myself and extremely critical of my behavior over the last few days. I was physically and emotionally sick.

Bobby and the kids left for church. When they returned, I was still in the bed. Bobby was still in a festive mood and allowed the kids to invite friends over to finish eating the Thanksgiving leftovers. Why on earth would he do that? I didn't want to hear any noise, smell food, or be bothered, so I lay in the bed in silence. I was angry at Bobby. Here I was lying in bed sick, and my husband couldn't attend to me because he had to serve and entertain the kids and their guests. About 9:00 PM, things started to settle down, and Bobby came back to the bedroom to check on me. I got up, took a shower, and changed the bed sheets. I kept repeating to myself, "This is the last night, by tomorrow they will be gone."

Everyone got up Monday morning and went off to school. I tried to begin my morning routine, but realized my energy level was still low from not eating; I didn't think I could make it a full day at work. I didn't like calling in sick, but I had no choice. Later that morning, I came out of my bedroom for the first time in two days, ate some crackers, and slowly began to feel better. I was grateful to have my house back and thankful Bobby was taking the kids home after school. Bobby checked on me around lunch and informed me of the proposed schedule for the evening. I asked about dinner, and he suggested lasagna or bratwursts. I considered it strange that he would suggest foods not recommended for someone recovering from a stomach virus. He continued to say he would have the kids start putting their clothes together so that when he took them to school in the morning everything would be ready to go. My end of the phone went silent; my mind was screaming, "Another night?" I managed to get off the phone with Bobby before I began screaming, "I can't take another night!" Immediately, my stomach began churning again, and I found myself back in the bathroom again off and on again for several hours. Somehow I made it through the evening, and by the time I came home from work the next day, they had returned to the bio-mom's house. My house and digestive system could return to normal.

Working in a health care environment for over fifteen years, I have heard physicians comment that most of the chronic diseases they treat day in and day out, including hypertension, chronic pain, diabetes, headaches, and depression, are all related to stress. In the science of stress research, connections have been shown between the mind and the immune system. Author and pastor, Michael Barry, after extensive medical, theological, and sociological research at the Philadelphia Cancer Treatment Centers of America, made a startling discovery: the immune system and forgiveness are very much connected. In his book, *The Forgiveness Project*, he states, "Chronic stress is beyond God's design for our bodies, it is the subject of numerous Bible passages, most of which have to do with avoiding worry and fear, and encouraging trust and joy" (Barry 2011, 85). Living-in-step is stressful all the way around; therefore it is important for you to find a way to relieve your anxiety and take care of yourself.

As far as my Graves' disease goes, I stayed in remission for about two years, and it came back with a vengeance in September of 2006. After resuming medication, I went back into remission for another six months. My endocrinologist continued to believe I had a pretty good chance of beating the disease. We celebrated and believed our prayers had been answered. However, the heart palpitations returned, so in July 2007, I gave up the hope of being healed and had my thyroid removed radioactively. As expected, four months later, my diagnosis changed to underactive thyroid which is much safer and easier to treat. My health is much better now, and I am committed to keeping my stress levels low through prayer, meditation, exercise, and eating right.

Stepmom Survival Tips

1. Acknowledge ambivalence up front and understand it can happen.
2. Understand that even though you love your stepchildren some days you may not like them.
3. Avoidance is not the answer. Don't try to constantly avoid your stepchildren.
4. Talk openly to your husband about your feelings.
5. Take care of your mental, physical, and emotional health.
6. Learn creative ways to deal with your stress. Find another stepmom for support who will allow you to vent. Offer a listening ear to another stepmom.
7. Overcome negative thoughts with prayer and positive affirmations.
8. Know your physiological symptoms when you are stressed.
9. Seek counseling as needed from a professional and/or visit your primary care physician.
10. Pray regularly about anxiety and find quiet time alone with God to discuss your fears.

Helpful Scriptures

I Peter 5:7 (NIV)
Cast all your anxiety on him because he cares for you.

John 14:27 (NIV)
Peace I leave with you; my peace I give you. I do not give to you as the world gives. Do not let your hearts be troubled and do not be afraid.

Philemon 1:6 (KJV)
That the communication of thy faith may become effectual by the acknowledging of every good thing which is in you in Christ Jesus.

Galatians 6:9 (NIV)
Let us not become weary in doing good, for at the proper time we will reap a harvest if we do not give up.

Proverbs 12:25 (NIV)
Anxiety weighs down the heart, but a kind word cheers it up.

John 11:4 (NIV)
When he heard this, Jesus said, "This sickness will not end in death. No, it is for God's glory so that God's Son may be glorified through it."

Chapter Ten
The Kitchen Wars

Better a dry crust with peace and quiet than a house full of feasting, with strife. Proverbs 17:1(NIV)

A House Divided

L iving-in-step had really become awful for us. We argued about the children, I avoided them as much as possible, and we drew biological lines in the sand. Neither Bobby nor I was in a good place. Once again, I sought the written advice of stepfamily experts to understand stepfamily dynamics. I soon learned that we had reached the stage of awareness and mobilization as reviewed in the book *Therapy with Stepfamilies* (Visher & Visher 1996).

Awareness – Growing awareness of family pressures. A stepparent begins to perceive what changes are needed. The parent feels pulled between the needs of children and of the new spouse. Groups divide along biological lines. Children may observe and exploit differences between the couple.

Mobilization – Strong emotions begin to be expressed, often leading to arguments between the couple. The stepparent is clear on the need for change. The biological parent fears change will bring loss. Sharp divisions exist between biological groups.

Why Are We Arguing About Food?

Bobby and I considered ourselves a fun loving couple. Early in our marriage, we were proud that we were rarely mad at each other and hardly ever argued. Because we had received so much opposition from others, we stood as a united force against the world. Nowadays, we were disagreeing regularly, with eighty percent of our quarrels involving discord related to our children. Our discussion may have been about something as simple as what time we were going to leave and eventually led to a dispute about something we had not intended to discuss.

One argument in particular, I could not believe we were having. Bobby and I were making decisions about our Thanksgiving celebration and easily agreed on a menu, guest list, and the starting time. Somehow our discussion led to what to do with the food immediately following the meal. Being raised by a mother who abided by food sanitation rules I learned not to leave poultry or any type of food out for more than a few hours; therefore, I commented that the food be stored in the refrigerator after everyone finished eating. Bobby on the other hand came from a family where everyone was coming and going at various times, rarely eating the dinner meal together. He was taught to leave the food in the oven until the last one ate and then his mother would return to the kitchen, no matter how late it was, to put the food away. By the way, Bobby didn't have any sisters, so his Mom did most of the work around the kitchen. Bobby listened to my confirmation, and then suggested leaving the food on the stove or in the oven so that everyone could help themselves when they were hungry again. He embraced watching others eating as much as they wanted and encouraged it. I had no problems with eating more food; I just didn't like leaving food out.

I firmly stated that once the meal was finished the leftovers be stowed in the refrigerator. Bobby followed my comments with a request. He was okay with my concerns about leaving the food out, but appealed to me to make the following announcement towards the end of the meal. "Even though we are putting up the food, you all are welcome to eat as much as you want, whenever you want to." I immediately questioned why I needed to make such a statement. He explained he didn't want anyone to think they were not welcome to the food or that they needed to hide because they wanted a piece of bread. I immediately took offense to his assertion because I believed he was insinuating I had a problem with his kids getting food when they were hungry. I asked him what he meant by his statement. He further explained, he wanted his kids to feel comfortable about eating and not have to ask permission to get food nor feel like they had to hide food whenever they got something without asking. His clarification did not help because at that point I was furious.

Just to show you how bad things can get when you are in the mobilization stage, before I knew it Bobby and I we were in a full blown argument about food. In fact, we argued about food from several different angles. Looking back now, we were arguing about FOOD! I could never have imagined arguing with anyone about what to eat, how to eat it, or when to eat it. However, being in the mobilization stage meant Bobby and I began to argue about various topics to defend ourselves and/or our children. Following are examples of the ridiculous arguments about food related topics that weren't so silly at the time.

Sunday Food Fight

When I was growing up, my mother encouraged us to get out of the bed on Sunday morning for church by cooking a wonderful breakfast consisting of homemade waffles. As I became a mother, I embraced preparing breakfast on Sunday mornings. My menu consisted of cinnamon rolls and blueberry muffins. After I had everything ready, and the aroma of food was in the air, I woke Aaron and Aiden up, hoping for a pleasant attitude. My behavior was consistent after Bobby and I married. On Sunday mornings I prepared enough to feed seven. In Bobby's previous marriage, mornings were a little more hectic, so their practice was to provide the kids with an assortment of cereals and let them have their choice for a quick simple breakfast.

We were talking one day when Bobby mentioned his kids were not used to eating a formal breakfast on Sunday mornings and asked him if they could eat cereal instead. As he explained why they preferred cereal, my thoughts centered on how ungrateful they were. I thought about my intentions in preparing breakfast and the time involved, so how could they be unappreciative for my cooking them a hot meal? My anger led to not wanting to cook anything for them. Every time I went into the kitchen while they were there, I reminded myself of their ingratitude. Bobby tried to appease me by having a discussion with them about being appreciative of my preparing breakfast for them on Sunday mornings. Bobby talking with them didn't help matters either because in their minds, now he was defending me.

Sunday afternoon meals were important to us. Bobby or I often prepared a big meal which almost always included a lot of meat and cornbread. One of my favorites was beef pot roast with potatoes and carrots, greens or green beans, macaroni and cheese, corn on the cob and cornbread. Because it was expensive to take seven people out to eat, we did not accept invitations out to dinner on kid weekends. Meal preparations began before we left for church. The cornbread was the only item left to prepare when we arrived home from church. My goal after arriving home was to have the food on the table within thirty minutes, ready to eat.

While putting the finishing touches on Sunday dinner, Bobby's kids on a few occasions entered the kitchen and searched the cabinet or the refrigerator for something to eat. After they located something, they opened it, reheated it if necessary, and sat at the counter and ate it. As I watched them out of the corner of my eye, I thought to myself,

"Don't you see me standing here cooking dinner?" It was obvious to anyone the food would be ready in a few moments. Sometimes the snack would be the pizza or Chinese food from the night before which didn't make sense to me. After observing this behavior, I established a new rule; no one was to go in the kitchen after we came home from church unless getting something to drink. On occasion, when the kids arrived home before us, they hurried and ate food from the previous night as soon as they got home. I believed this behavior to be complete defiance. I tried to explain I had no problems with anyone going in the kitchen any other time and getting whatever they wanted. Just don't do it when I am cooking the meal we are about to eat.

Assumptions

One Sunday morning during kid weekend, my children were gone to the bio-dad's house for a special occasion. I woke up with a headache, so Bobby instructed his children to eat cereal before going to church. I took some meds, went back to bed, woke up later, put dinner in the oven, and headed to church. The next time we had a Sunday morning in which my children were gone, a strange phenomenon happened. As usual, I was in the kitchen preparing breakfast and dinner simultaneously. On any given Sunday, we had to wake up all of the kids, but for some reason Bobby's kids were already up. My kitchen routine started around 7:00 AM and I woke the kids up usually around 7:45 to 8:00. As I was cooking, suddenly all three of Bobby's children said good morning and then prepared a bowl of cereal for themselves.

There was no way they had awakened on their own so I went upstairs to ask Bobby why he woke them up so early when breakfast wasn't ready yet. Bobby informed me of his assumption that since my children were not at home, he needed to do everything for his children. I asked him what he based this assumption on. He mentioned it had happened before when my daughter wasn't at home.

I couldn't believe he was insinuating that I was not going to feed his children because mine were not home. I finished getting dressed and went to the kitchen to throw all of the food I had prepared in the trash. I refused to come home from church and see uneaten breakfast food sitting on the counter. Anger and frustration consumed me, and I needed to get out the house immediately, but I had nowhere to go. Sunday school didn't start for another hour. As a couple, we had a rule that we didn't argue on Sunday mornings. I never wanted to disrupt the Lord's work and cause Bobby to be angry while delivering his sermon. However, I had to get out because the children would have seen the strain between Bobby and me. Somehow I ended up in the driveway of the house we were planning to purchase. I sat in the car for about 40 minutes, praying about whether or not it was God's will for us to move our problems to a new house.

By the time we came home, we were not speaking to each other, and I did everything I could to not be in a group situation. I came home, finished preparing dinner, and announced dinner was ready. Although I was hungry, I had to excuse myself. I went upstairs and waited until later to eat. When Bobby returned from taking his children home, the squabble began.

The Last Straw

Bobby had always taught his children to say thank you after meals; therefore, anytime we ate a meal at our house, his children always said thank you for the food when they got up from the table. This was a practice I had taught my children to say when visiting other's homes, but a thank you was not required in our home. In the beginning, I was flattered that Bobby's children thanked me for cooking. The problem came when I started to believe they were saying it out of fear. The events occurred in this order. One child said, "Thank you," and the other two or three jumped to attention immediately to repeat, "Thank you," as well. It was almost as if they were going to get in trouble if they didn't. After a while I viewed a thank you as patronizing and no longer felt like it was coming from the heart.

One weekend during a low period for me, Bobby's kids came over and I found myself perturbed and feeling unappreciated. They used the phone whenever they wanted to, washed several loads of clothes, and left lights and televisions on all over the house. They did not even appreciate everything that I sacrificed so that their father could be a hero in their eyes. After dinner, all of the kids specifically thanked Bobby for the dinner, but neglected to say thank you to me. The issue wasn't about who cooked the meal; it was about who had sacrificed to make the meal possible. I didn't say anything, but stewed on the inside. I wanted to do something crazy like throw all the food in the air and just walk out the house. I was saddened by the way our lives had turned out. That's when something inside me screamed, "We have to do something!"

Family life was awful. We were arguing more and more, and it was taking longer to make up. Sometimes we went several days barely speaking to one another or not speaking at all. We still prayed together in the morning, but that was the extent of communication between us. I felt like an ignored, emotionally abused outsider, living in my own home. As I tried to explain my feelings to Bobby, he was too consumed with his own feelings. I complained to him about his kids, and they complained to him about me. We even began to compare children. All conversations concerning our children ended in an argument or an impasse. By the time we recovered from a kid weekend, which now took a week, it was time for visitation to happen all over again.

Bobby felt like he was in the middle and couldn't do anything to fix our troubles. He felt useless for not being able to help any of us, not even himself and soon became emotionally paralyzed. As he began to shut down, I blamed him for not being able to control his children and protect me. Bobby saw how discouraged I was and said he had done all he could to help our situation. Bobby talked about the poison pill he felt like the bio-mom had dropped on the children to be the force causing dissention between us. The children had to take the side of the bio-mom, and I was expendable. I could not believe we had reached a point that allowed someone else to control our home.

I Can't Do This Anymore

I almost didn't include this section in this book because I really didn't want Bobby to know how bad things became for me. I'm not sure he ever really knew I had thoughts about ending our marriage. Divorce sounded like the best answer for the misery we were experiencing. The hopes of being one big happy family were gone forever. It was a myth. The Brady Bunch was not attainable. We were between years three and four when I found myself daydreaming for life the way it used to be. I was wishing, hoping, and praying for peace in our marriage, but nothing was changing for the better.

As I had experienced in my first marriage, a marriage relationship is tough to sustain. Statistics show that it doesn't get easier the second time around. Second marriages are even less likely to survive than a first marriage. In reality, almost two thirds of second marriages end in divorce. Furthermore, data conveys that seventy percent of second marriages involving stepchildren fail. According to the Stepfamily Foundation, the median duration of second marriages that end in divorce for males is 7.3 years, for women 6.8 years (Lofas, 2004). I understood why these were unsuccessful and wondered how they made it up to seven or eight years.

Anne Kass, a retired District Judge of Albuquerque, New Mexico stated, that "These marriages fail for a number of reasons. One is there often are ongoing money problems from the first divorce. Another, more common cause of second marriages failing is these new families' lives get so complicated. Maintaining human relationships is a hard task. As the number of relationships increases, the opportunities for conflict grow, and the task of keeping the peace gets more difficult each and every day" (Kass n.d.). I knew we were in trouble if we didn't do something fast. Divorce was not really an option, but it sounded like a great solution because I didn't see any hope for our family. I loved Bobby and wanted to stay married, but I had given up hope on staying together if we continued to have the ongoing tension in our home.

Broken Promises

When I first made the decision to marry Bobby, I made a promise to him that I would never come between him and his children. Never would I believe in a million years our marriage would suffer because of my inability to build a positive relationship with his children. The fear of loss began to consume Bobby; he was afraid of losing me and afraid of losing his children. To save our marriage, Bobby began to push the children in the opposite direction; back towards their mother who he felt like was strongly influencing their behavior. He began to limit their interactions with me to ease some of the tension in our home.

To give us a break and to regroup, I suggested we change our weekend visitation schedule so we would not have our kids the same weekend. My plan was to parent my child as usual the weekends she was with us, and then leave the house the entire weekend when Bobby's kids visited. I wasn't sure where I would go; I just didn't want to be in the house when they were there. My rationale was that Bobby could spend time with his children without my interference, and I could have peace. This idea didn't feel like a good option for Bobby, because he would be totally responsible for their care, without my assistance. It would be difficult for him to manage with his schedule. Besides, Bobby didn't want me to feel like I was being kicked out of my own home. Worst of all, giving up our alone weekends, would lessen the time we had to spend alone, which could make matters even more dreadful.

I had given up hope, and then out of fear and frustration I made a very harsh decision, but it clearly shows how desperate I was. I recommended that we decline our weekend visitation rights with his children every other weekend until we could fix our marriage. To make sure he maintained his relationship with them, I suggested he spend more time with them during the week such as picking them up from school, and finding creative ways to parent without them staying over the weekend.

I knew I was taking a huge risk demanding the change, but if we didn't do something, my next step was to work towards a temporary separation of households. I suggested he speak with the bio-mom regarding her contribution to the children's behavior and inform her we would not be picking them up on the weekends until they learned to be respectful of our marriage and me as their stepmother. If he didn't feel comfortable having the conversation, I was willing to do it myself, since it was primarily my decision.

I knew Bobby was doing his best to fix the situation with me and be a good parent at the same time. According to Stormie Omartian's book, *The Power of a Praying Wife*, one of her husband's deepest fears was the fear of not being a good father. Bobby too had this fear and not hosting them regularly would deepen his apprehension. I also feared that if I were the reason why he felt like he was not a good father that he would one day come to resent me.

Following my risky decision to cancel biweekly visitation, Bobby and I intensely focused on our marriage and attempted to regroup. We prayed for wisdom and strength while I also focused my prayers on Bobby's relationship with his children. He soon found even more creative ways to spend time with his children, such as picking them up from school, going on outings during the weekend, and planned vacations. I was grateful for his efforts and determination to repair our marriage.

Stepmom Survival Tips

1. Discuss problems and differences head on and don't allow them to simmer.
2. Do not be resentful when stepchildren prefer the traditions and rituals of their former intact family.
3. Don't sweat the small stuff. Believe me; a lot of it is small.
4. Learn to compromise and ask the stepchildren for their preferences on occasion.
5. Recognize when your marriage is in trouble.
6. Get help from a professional counselor.
7. Do not let divorce enter your thoughts or conversations.
8. Make decisions together. (Even simple ones like menu preparation during visitation.)
9. Ease up on some of the household rules that really don't make a difference.
10. Be willing to explain why you prefer things a certain way.
11. In order to survive as a stepmom, you need thick skin. Don't take everything personally.

Helpful Scriptures

Luke 21:34 (NIV)
"Be careful, or your hearts will be weighed down with dissipation, drunkenness and the anxieties of life, and that day will close on you suddenly like a trap.

Proverbs 25:21 (NIV)
If your enemy is hungry, give him food to eat; if he is thirsty, give him water to drink.

Romans 12:19-21 (NIV)
Do not take revenge, my dear friends, but leave room for God's wrath, for it is written: "It is mine to avenge; I will repay," says the Lord. On the contrary: "If your enemy is hungry, feed him; if he is thirsty, give him something to drink. In doing this, you will heap burning coals on his head." Do not be overcome by evil, but overcome evil with good.

Hosea 14:4 (NIV)
I will heal their waywardness and love them freely, for my anger has turned away from them.

1 Samuel 1:7-8 (NIV)
This went on year after year. Whenever Hannah went up to the house of the LORD, her rival provoked her till she wept and would not eat. Elkanah her husband would say to her, "Hannah, why are you weeping? Why don't you eat? Why are you downhearted? Don't I mean more to you than ten sons?"

Chapter Eleven
I Love Them, I Love Them Not

My dear children, I write this to you so that you will not sin. But if anybody does sin, we have one who speaks to the Father in our defense — Jesus Christ, the Righteous One. I John 2:1-2 (NIV)

The Word is Sharper than a Two Edged Sword

On Sunday morning, February 11, 2007, I sat on the second row, in my usual seat, and listened to Bobby preach a sermon entitled, "When I Come Out, I'm Going to Be a Blessing." The sermon was taken from II Corinthians 12:6-9, where Paul shared his struggles concerning the thorn in his flesh and how he had asked the Lord to remove it three times. I am attentive to Bobby's sermons and can constantly find something to enhance my Christian walk. As usual, I was recording notes in my journal as he gave his sermon points. No doubt in my twenty-three years as a born again Christian, I had heard this scripture preached by many ministers. In addition, I am sure I had taught this scripture in Sunday school.

As Bobby continued his sermon, I slowly came to the realization that Paul and I had the same problem. I too had a thorn that would not go away, no matter how much I had prayed. My thorn was my poor relationship with my stepchildren. Like Paul, no matter how many times Bobby and I had prayed about it together and separately, we weren't making any progress. We had been praying for four years and had other prayer warriors praying for us. However, God had reminded me all along "his grace was sufficient." Although I know God is able to do anything, we were at the end of our rope, and I was hanging on by a very thin emotional thread on the verge of breaking.

I Can't Cry

I often refrain from crying in church because as the pastor's wife, my sorrow begins a guessing game of what could be the cause of my distress. There's a strong assumption that when the first lady cries, it is commonly the pastor's fault, and there is something wrong with the marriage. Physically, I suffer from dry eye disease, meaning it is difficult for me to make tears. It's probably for the best because I don't consider myself a beautiful crier. In the movies, Halle Berry always looks beautiful when she cries, but I am not one of those people. On that particular Sunday, the timing wasn't right either because we were having a leadership meeting immediately following church. There would not be enough time to run home and re-apply makeup. I require several hours to recover from crying, and it usually involves a wet compress over my eyes, followed by some sleep.

Despite my determination to not cry, it was extremely difficult for me to make it through the rest of the service without the tears falling. It was very obvious by my red eyes and nose I had been crying. I put on my prescription glasses so that hopefully no one would notice. All I wanted to do was go home, climb into the bed, curl up into a ball, and have a really good cry. I looked over at Sister Young, one of the senior ladies (also a stepmom), who knew my plight. I daydreamed about putting my head on her shoulder, crying some more, and hearing her tell me, "It's going to be all right."

As I sat there, I asked the Holy Spirit to reveal to me what my problem was and why I had not been able to fix the situation. A word of caution, be careful what you ask for because you may not be able to handle the truth. The answer suddenly hit me like a brick wall. The Spirit revealed to me the reason our lives were in such turmoil was because I couldn't admit that even though I loved my stepchildren, I really didn't like them. I said to myself, this can't be true, I love everybody. I had just finished singing along during devotion, "I will trust in the Lord, and I'm going to treat everybody right, until I die." I spoke the words out loud to myself, "I don't like my stepchildren." The words rolled off of my tongue so well, I said them a few more times. It sounds harsh, but admitting it somehow made me feel better. After all, in a twelve step program for addicts, it is only when one admits he has a problem that the recovery and healing process can begin.

How were we going to survive this marriage when I didn't like his children? In the book *Parenting the Other Chick's Eggs*, Ruth Ann Clurman reminds stepfamilies that it is not usually love at first sight for stepparents and stepchildren. She asks the questions: "How do you find warmth in a strange nest when you honestly can't say you love the other birds? How can you tolerate these avian imposters without pecking at each other when you don't even really like them" (Clurman 1997, 40)?

I couldn't understand how or when my intentions and feelings reversed. In the beginning of our marriage, I knew his children didn't like having me for a stepmom and often did things causing me great disappointment. However, I kept on loving and giving. Somewhere along the way, I had given up trying, because every act of kindness I tried showed little improvement in their behavior. They had caused me much pain by not accepting my love. I learned to stop trying and as a result refused to give them the opportunity to hurt me anymore. I wanted them to feel the pain of rejection. Now I was the one who was not living in God's will and refusing to love!

Baby, What's Wrong?

Bobby came home from church and knew something was wrong with me. I was hurting too much to talk about it and needed some time alone. He went ahead and finished cooking dinner, but I didn't have an appetite. Being concerned, he asked what happened. I told him I was better, but I needed to talk to him about something. Because we didn't have to be anywhere, I knew the Lord had provided this time for us truly to share with one another. I started the conversation by thanking him for the sermon he had preached and explained my interpretation of the thorn in my flesh being his kids. I then explained to him as gently as possible that I realized I didn't like his children, and I had felt that way for some time. I tried to explain by describing an event that happened the day before.

I usually don't work Saturdays, but on this particular occasion, I had to work all day, and was on my feet for the entire time. As I was leaving work, I called Bobby to let him know how my day went and that I was on my way home. As we were talking, there was a lot of background noise and I soon realized his kids were at the house. Part of me was frustrated because he could have warned me, but he was doing just what I had asked him to do by spending time with them when I was out of the house. After realizing the kids were there, I immediately tensed up and began to think of other things to do besides going home. Extreme fatigue and my aching feet quickly reminded me that all I had the energy to do was go home and take an afternoon nap. Because I knew I was uneasy, I whispered a short prayer and repeated positive self-talk to convince myself to have "happy thoughts" prepared for my arrival home. I even took the long way around to prepare myself.

As soon as I walked in the door, my attitude took over immediately, and I wanted nothing to do with either Bobby or the kids. I went straight to our bedroom, took off my shoes, climbed into the bed, and fell asleep. Thirty minutes later, Bobby was ready to take the kids home. Not knowing I was sleeping, he encouraged the kids to come upstairs and say goodbye. Sleep was more important and I didn't want to be bothered. I mumbled "bye" through the door as they knocked on it one at a time. I didn't bother to get up because it wouldn't make a difference anyway.

I tried to explain my feelings and behavior to Bobby and why it bothered me so much that the kids were at the house when I came home. I rationalized that if I had a warning I may have been better. The entire time I explained my position to him, I knew it wasn't fair for Bobby to have to ask my permission to bring his children to the house unannounced. I was just tired of feeling uncomfortable in my own home when they were around.

Confession is Good for the Soul

I poured my heart out to Bobby and acknowledged I needed help, but I didn't know where to start. Bobby thanked me for admitting how I felt and agreed my actions had spoken loudly. He went on to talk about a time when he had encouraged the kids to bond with me, and they had come back and told him I wasn't interested. He talked about how he found himself in a difficult situation and how he and the kids had tried. Somehow, after pouring out my heart and soul, that was not quite what I wanted to hear. What I wanted to hear was "Thank you for sharing baby, and whatever you need from me to get through this, I am here for you. Now let us pray."

Instead, it was obvious Bobby had a few complaints to get off of his chest too. He acknowledged having tried everything he could think of and was tired of being in the middle trying to control everyone. He also explained his kids were good kids, and they had often told him about things my kids did or didn't do and what I did and didn't do. At this point I couldn't hold it any longer and said, "You know when a person admits that they have sinned, it is not the time to list additional sins as you remember them, but to accept the apology and move forward."

I was sorry I had shared and wanted to go back to working it out with the Lord. My emotions got the best of me, and I reminded him of all the turmoil I had received from his side of the fence. I welled up again and spent two hours crying my eyes out on his chest and complained of all the terrible things his family, the church, the district, his friends, or anyone else had done to me since we married. I was hurting in a way that no one could heal my emotional wounds.

The conversation had not worked out as I had planned. I felt judged and hurt. My pain turned into anger towards Bobby. After a long period of crying and then complete silence, Bobby could sense my emotional agony. He was moved with compassion and apologized for his response, and we talked until I fell asleep. We agreed to pray more focused prayers and come up with a plan for our family to heal.

The Wicked Stepmother

The fairy tale expression "wicked stepmother" is alive and well, even today. One of the reasons I didn't like the name stepmom, was because it so often had the adjectives evil or wicked attached to it. Was I turning into the wicked stepmother? It was a label I had promised myself I would never be. In preparing to be a stepmom, I had watched a couple of movies presenting the stepmom as an evil being. I couldn't imagine a woman even thinking about mistreating children. That would never be me!

I searched the internet for the label "wicked stepmother" and found numerous pictures and images of Cinderella's stepmom and the like. Many blogs have been written by frustrated women who had been cast into this role. The internet is full of stepmoms reaching out for help and trying to explain why they feel the way they do about their marriages and their stepchildren. Many give up and decide life was much better before the marriage. Again, no wonder 70% of second marriages fail when there are children involved.

There is nothing in literature or fairy tales to present stepfathers in a negative light. He is often seen as prince charming who has come to rescue the single mom from a life of misery and poverty. On the other hand, the stepmom is known as the wicked witch who rode in on her vacuum, sucked Dad into the marriage, and was threatening to ship the rascals to boarding school on the other side of the country.

According to the Stepfamily Foundation, one of the most common complaints of stepmoms is the feeling you are turning into the "cruel" stepmother. In Jeannette Lofas' book entitled *Stepparenting*, she states, "Stepmothers were never born with 'cruel' on their passport, but it's easy to become that way, given the dynamics of Step relationships" (Lofas 2004, 41). Laura Petherbridge in *The Smart Stepmom* stated, "There's a reason stepmoms get to this point. While you may be married to the best husband in the world, the complications of a stepfamily can bring out the worst - even in a godly, determined stepmom" (Deal and Petherbridge 2009, 52).

Being Honest with Yourself

It was not easy for me to admit my feelings had changed towards my stepchildren and that I could be labeled "cruel" based on my behavior. I was the one who no longer desired a relationship and wanted to push them away. I blamed them and asked myself how they could be so unloving and ungrateful? I even felt resentment towards Bobby for not making them love and respect me. How could he raise kids who treated adults with disdain? I attempted to justify my behavior by keeping account of the many acts of kindness that I had shown toward them along with a record of their injustices towards me.

The most difficult concept to accept was that I wasn't "Janice, the Super Stepmom" who magically made my stepchildren love me. I was disappointed we weren't going to be the model stepfamily showing everybody how it should be done. Our testimony was ruined, and other families would lose hope. Public opinion mattered, but I needed to be pleasing in God's sight as being loving and forgiving. The truth is, being around my stepchildren caused me to realize how powerless I was over their love and their behavior. Rejection was not easy for me, especially when I was working so hard and giving so much love. Not being able to control them caused me to become more demanding.

In the *Stepfamily Survival Guide*, Natalie Nichols Gillespie shared, "Stepparents may find themselves disillusioned quickly in a new marriage when children who started out as loving angels, as friends, quickly become the enemy after they officially become your stepchildren" (Gillespie 2004, 91). She was absolutely right, we were so disillusioned. I thought they adored me when we were dating and in the beginning of our marriage. It had come to a point where I was wounded and wanted to lash out at the source of my pain. I wanted them to hurt like I did, so I made the decision to treat them as they had treated me. As I pondered our situation, I felt terrible and couldn't believe our relationship had come to this.

Lord, Please Help Me

The knowledge of how I truly felt about my stepchildren was an awakening for me, and I knew just what had to be done to move forward. After hearing's Bobby's sermon, I went home from church and after spending a couple hours crying and praying, I asked the Lord to forgive me and acknowledged I needed help. I had to seek His forgiveness and direction before speaking with Bobby. Our Sunday school lesson for the week came out of John 11 where Jesus had the conversation with Martha about Lazarus' death. She told Jesus that if he had been there her brother would not have died. Because she had a relationship with Jesus and faith in his ability to do anything, Jesus raised Lazarus from the dead. After thinking about it and praying, my situation wasn't anywhere as challenging as raising someone from the dead, even though it seemed like it would take a miracle to heal our situation. I realized even though I was afraid, nothing was too hard for God. I would have to lean on this truth in order to restore and rebuild.

Stepmom Survival Tips

1. Accept the fact that love is usually not instant in stepfamilies.
2. Be honest with yourself about how you really feel. Admit it and move forward.
3. Do not beat up on yourself for not instantly loving your stepchildren or for disliking them.
4. Talk to your husband about your feelings without blaming him or the children.
5. In speaking with your husband about your feelings, remind him that you need him to listen, not to judge you, or solve the problem for you.
6. There is healing in confiding in others. Find someone who understands. Share with another stepmom and seek solutions together.
7. You do not have to become "wicked" because you have been hurt.
8. Read stepfamily books and blogs to understand that you are not the first stepmom to feel this way.
9. Share resources and information with your spouse.
10. Ask for God's forgiveness and help to love and forgive your stepchildren.

Helpful Scriptures

2 Corinthians 12:8-9 (NIV)

Three times I pleaded with the Lord to take it away from me. But he said to me, "My grace is sufficient for you, for my power is made perfect in weakness. Therefore I will boast all the more gladly about my weaknesses, so that Christ's power may rest on me.

James 5:16 (NIV)

Therefore confess your sins to each other and pray for each other so that you may be healed. The prayer of a righteous person is powerful and effective.

Nehemiah 9:2 (NIV)

Those of Israelite descent had separated themselves from all foreigners. They stood in their places and confessed their sins and the sins of their ancestors.

Psalm 38:4 (NIV)

My guilt has overwhelmed me like a burden too heavy to bear.

Psalm 51:10 (NIV)

Create in me a pure heart, O God, and renew a steadfast spirit within me.

1 John 2:1-2 (NIV)

My dear children, I write this to you so that you will not sin. But if anybody does sin, we have an advocate with the Father – Jesus Christ, the Righteous One. He is the atoning sacrifice for our sins, and not only for ours but also for the sins of the whole world.

Chapter Twelve

The Path to Forgiveness

Hatred stirs up dissension, but love covers over all wrongs.
Proverbs 10:12 (NIV)

Acknowledging I needed God's help to forgive myself as well as my husband and stepchildren was the first step towards healing. Monday morning, following my tearful conversation with Bobby regarding my dislike for his children, I woke up with a determination to mend our broken relationships. The alarm went off at the usual 5:00 AM, and my eyes were still puffy from all of the crying I had done the day before. During my morning devotion and Bible study, I was led to Ephesians 4:31-32. "Let all bitterness, and wrath and anger and clamour, and evil speaking, be put away from you, with all malice. And be ye kind to one another, tenderhearted, forgiving one another even as God for Christ's sake hath forgiven you."

Scripture was what I needed to begin the plan to restore myself, my relationship with Bobby's kids and most of all my marriage to Bobby. After spending time in prayer, it was revealed that forgiveness was in order. It was vital I begin to forgive his children for the things done early in the marriage leading us down the path of destruction. Also, while sitting in my office, I scanned my library, looking through religious books for anything on forgiveness. I was led to a book by

Cheryl Richardson, *The Unmistakable Touch of Grace*. In chapter four entitled "Who Are Your Spiritual Change Agents?" I found the following statement, "Sometimes the people who have the most powerful effect on our lives are the ones who cause us the most pain" (Richarson 2005, 101). In the resource section of her book, there was a book listed in the resource section entitled, *Dare to Forgive* by Dr. Edward Hallowell. His book provides an honest and loving look at the path to forgiveness. Before I knew it, I was on Amazon.com, ordered the book, and couldn't wait for it to be delivered. However, I knew the answer to everything could be found in the bible so I began to look for every scripture I could find related to forgiveness. The first scripture I came across was:

> **Genesis 50:15-21 (NIV)**
> *When Joseph's brothers saw that their father was dead, they said, "What if Joseph holds a grudge against us and pays us back for all the wrongs we did to him?" So they sent word to Joseph, saying, "Your father left these instructions before he died: 'This is what you are to say to Joseph: I ask you to forgive your brothers the sins and the wrongs they committed in treating you so badly.' Now please forgive the sins of the servants of the God of your father." When their message came to him, Joseph wept. His brothers then came and threw themselves down before him. "We are your slaves," they said. But Joseph said to them, "Don't be afraid. Am I in the place of God? You intended to harm me, but God intended it for good to accomplish what is now being done, the saving of many lives. So then, don't be afraid. I will provide for you and your children." And he reassured them and spoke kindly to them.*

See how the Lord works? This scripture is one that Bobby had mentioned in his sermon on yesterday. Joseph's brothers intended to do harm to him when they left him for dead. Regarding our situation, I believed harm was intended to me because they were hurting from realizing their parents would never get back together; however, God intended it for my good. Now I can tell my story and help someone else who may be going through the same turmoil of living-in-step.

Dr. Hallowell, in *Dare to Forgive,* (Hallowell 2004, 157), discussed forgiveness occurring in 4 phases: 1) pain and hurt 2) reliving and reflecting 3) working it out, and 4) taking stock and moving forward.

Because I had been unwilling to forgive, my life and marriage became a mess. My physical health suffered, and to this day, I believe my Graves' disease was related to the stress I was experiencing in our stepfamily. My spiritual life also suffered because I knew I was supposed to be a model for others; instead, I was ruining my testimony. As I taught my Sunday school class on the topic of loving one another, I was convicted. I had managed to maintain an image of being happy and optimistic with a contagious positive attitude, but when I was in the presence of my stepchildren, I became someone with much different qualities, including low energy, negativity, and anger. There were times when my daughter Aiden asked me if I was mad or what was wrong.

I soon recognized I had not been able to forgive my stepchildren because they had caused me emotional pain. They had tolerated me, ignored me, and made it clear to me that their lives were much better before I came along and they didn't want or need a stepmother. Whether I wanted to admit it or not, I was hurt, and pain was the result. I thought I had tough skin. After all, I had endured many personal attacks over the course of my life and survived them all, moving forward even stronger.

In the beginning, I let my pain turn into revenge, but the Holy Spirit reminded me that through my grief, I may be able to help someone else. I wanted my sorrow to turn into a blessing for others. Instead, my pain was turning into misery for everyone. After spending time focusing on forgiveness, I realized that prayer alone was not going to get me through the forgiveness process. I had to pray for the desire to forgive and then make some deliberate choices to begin the process. I desired to begin by trying to build positive memories with Bobby's kids.

Bio-Mom, Can We Work Together?

I had discussed earlier that my ex-husband and I agreed to do whatever we needed to do to show our children and others that even though we could not be married anymore; we could show courtesy and respect for one another and do what was needed for our children. Our courtesy continued when he remarried, for I respect and support his new wife. My daughter recently graduated from high school and we hosted a joint graduation celebration for her in our home and shared the expenses. We all sat together at graduation, and I attended his church with both of my children to celebrate her accomplishments. We would not have been able to work together if we had not agreed to put our differences aside, and co-parent our children.

I read somewhere that even after five years, some ex-wives are still angry at their ex-husbands. Although I had seen this behavior in other women, I couldn't imagine still trying to pick a fight with the bio-dad. We didn't argue in front of the children when we were married, and we weren't going to start this behavior after we divorced. Not that Bobby and the bio-mom argued a lot, but their inability to communicate and work together only made our situation worse. I decided to take things into my own hands and try to fix the dissention with the bio-mom. Most people would prefer to have nothing to do with their spouse's ex, but I knew trying to talk to her couldn't make matters any worse. The following week, I made a call to the bio-mom suggesting we meet for lunch or dinner. She declined the face-to-face meeting but agreed to speak with me by phone. My proposed agenda included the following topics:

- Try to forgive one another
- Stop bringing up the past and move forward
- Building a cordial relationship with her

- Demonstrate courtesy and respect to one another in the kids' presence
- Encourage her and Bobby to work together
- Strengthen her support system by helping out with the kids more and resuming visitation.

As we spoke, I explained my relationship was not what I desired with the kids, and I believed this was caused by the lack of communication and cordiality between us. I explained that on various occasions, our kids, in-laws, friends and relatives, felt awkward whenever she, Bobby, and I were forced to be in the same location together. It was obvious to everyone present that there was a huge elephant in the room, and we reacted by retreating to our respective corners. She expressed that she had no intentions for us to be friends or running buddies. I assured her my thoughts centered on us being cordial, with the ability to communicate effectively in support of the children.

We spent time talking about old wounds and how we may have offended one another. She also shared disappointment regarding Bobby's behavior and his decision to get married before the kids had time to adjust to the divorce. We both agreed that forgiveness was in order. She concluded she had already forgiven Bobby and apologized to him; however, he did not reciprocate. I shared my prayer for her and Bobby to be able to co-parent. To encourage her, I shared the mutual agreement my ex-husband and I have to support our children by being kind to one another and working together. I offered myself as a mediator for her and Bobby to communicate better for the children's sake.

During one of our conversations, she asked me point blank if I loved her children. I responded by attempting to explain the challenges I faced with them, particularly when all of them were together. I explained, "When they are together, they tend to shut me out." I also shared I would have never believed everything would have turned out this way, and my prayer and hope for her when she remarried was to have a good relationship with her stepchildren.

We had approximately four conversations, which lasted a minimum of an hour each. We made an agreement to move forward and leave the past behind us. Some positive results came from our conversations. According to their divorce decree, Bobby was responsible for health insurance, which I carried for the family. The bio-mom had not felt comfortable trusting me to be responsible for her children's insurance. I assured her they were covered, and I would send insurance cards. She could save money by not paying additional insurance premiums for them. I felt like we at least understood one another better, and I had an opportunity to express my desire for us to have a functional relationship for the kids' sake. Our efforts came to a screeching halt soon after she and Bobby had an angry discussion regarding money. Two steps forward, four steps back. Oh well, I tried.

Happy Graduation

One evening Janae, Bobby's oldest daughter, called the house phone. I answered the phone located in my office which does not have caller ID. As soon as I realized she was the caller, I assumed she wanted to speak with Bobby. He was at the church so I suggested she call back later; however, she continued to talk sharing her excitement about her new job, company car, and apartment. She was planning a house warming/graduation party and wanted my opinion on a few things. We had a great conversation, and I congratulated her for graduating from college and beginning a career.

As the party weekend approached, Janae wasn't feeling well physically. In her youth, she had suffered from spinal meningitis, the deadly kind. She recently had surgery and was experiencing some symptoms related to meningitis, including a headache and difficulty moving her neck. She called her doctor, described her symptoms, and was encouraged to go immediately to the emergency room. Bobby and I were out to dinner and had ignored our cell phones. When we got in the car to go home, we both checked our messages. We had the same message from Janae indicating she was in the emergency room at a nearby hospital, running tests.

We headed straight to the hospital and found Janae and a girlfriend in fairly good spirits. I was wondering why the bio-mom wasn't there because I was sure she would be worried. The bio-mom had been busy preparing for the graduation celebration scheduled for the next day. After we had been there for about an hour, the bio-mom showed up with two of the children and the mother of the friend present with Janae. She didn't seem overly concerned or alarmed and sat down across from us and discussed the party preparations. All of the tests ordered came back negative. Thank God. The staff informed Janae that the only real way to rule out meningitis was by doing an MRI and a spinal tap. The bio-mom and I had agreed that her situation didn't seem bad enough to warrant a spinal tap, but Janae wanted to rule out meningitis so they went ahead and ran both tests.

While we were waiting for Janae to return from the MRI, other family members began to arrive at the hospital. The younger children had not eaten so I offered to take them to get a sandwich. When I returned, the bio-mom was appreciative and the room actually felt comfortable. We had a decent conversation and focused on Janae. Only four people could be in the room with Janae, and many of her family members were waiting in the lobby. Her family and even Bobby was surprised to hear we were in the room together with no fireworks and actually being cordial to one another.

Again, the tests came back negative, and the bio-mom and I worked together to get Janae dressed and back home. When we left the hospital, it was 3:00 in the morning, and the jury was still out on whether or not to have the graduation party. When Bobby and I arrived home, we discussed the evening's events. He could not believe the positive interactions between the bio-mom and me. We agreed that it was a good thing to have the emergency room episode because it would help reduce the anxiety we were having about the graduation party in a few hours.

Morning came, and Janae was feeling better and up and around, so the party was still on. Janae called, and we agreed to bring the additional items needed for the party. We arrived early enough to help decorate and prepare. The bio-mom had stepped out to get dressed and returned to find me busy and greeted me kindly. As the guests arrived, we conversed off and on to let our guests know there was no hostility between us. It turned out to be a nice evening, and the bio-mom thanked me for helping out with the occasion. I can't remember the interactions between Bobby and the bio-mom, but he did have to admit my telephone efforts to build a relationship with the bio-mom perhaps made a difference after all. From then on, it was much easier to be in the same room. After she became engaged and then finally married, some of the pressure was lifted. Bobby made every effort to be cordial with his children's new stepfather.

Common Interests

Whenever you focus on looking for differences, you will most definitely find what you are looking for. The longer I thought about what was different about our two families, the more our differences pulled us apart. As an experienced trainer, I have taught diversity classes on many occasions. One exercise we do during the training encourages participants to look for similarities they have with others instead of focusing on differences. The instructions for the exercise are for everyone in the room to speak and share with as many people as possible in the room and list the things you have in common. Whoever listed the most similarities with others in the room was the winner. The rule was, however, you could not list visual similarities which were obvious, but to go beneath the surface and discover what was inside the person.

If I were deliberate, I could begin to find things in common with each of Bobby's children. I often reminded them we had one thing in common: we all love Bobby and need him in our lives. We also loved God and wanted him to be pleased with us. I looked for ways to find our commonalities and found each one of the Love children to be unique individuals with equally unique interests. As I reached out to them, small miracles began to happen.

One-by-One

I was deliberate in attempts to build one-on-one relationships with Bobby's children. I started with his daughter Jamie who was about to have a birthday. When the day arrived, I placed an early morning call to wish her a happy birthday. She was pleasantly surprised. I made some small talk and wished her a good day. As soon I delivered Bobby's morning coffee to him, I encouraged him to call her. I did not tell him I had already called.

About a week later, I called the bio-mom for her permission to invite Jamie to lunch to celebrate her birthday. We planned the outing for a Saturday two weeks later. I promised to arrive around 11:30 to pick her up. I woke with excitement and was determined to have a great lunch outing. We went to a great little boutique restaurant called Andre's, a Suisse confectionary, and had a fabulous time. The restaurant was perfect for a girls' day out and had the most incredible selection of chocolates and desserts. Jamie was surprised and enthused, stating she had never been to a place like Andre's.

During our fancy four course meal, we talked about her participation in the drill team and upcoming track season, hair and beauty products, and anything else Jamie wanted to talk about. I intentionally did not talk about anything negative or anything that could later be misinterpreted as questioning her. Most of all, I did not talk about our status as a stepfamily. Two hours later, we bought some extra deserts and headed backed to her house. I continued to keep the conversation neutral. Upon our departing, I gave her a hug, and she thanked me for the birthday lunch. I recommended we needed to try to spend more time together. She agreed.

Writing Letters

Next, I desired to speak with Brayden, but knew he wasn't much of a talker. I thought about a face to face meeting with him, but I didn't want to put pressure on him to talk to me. Forcing him to spend time with me one on one would only make matters worse for him. We purchased a cell phone for him as a Christmas gift, so I thought about calling him on his cell phone. Again, even a phone call would be terrifying for him. In the book *The Stepfamily Survival Guide*, author Natalie Nichols Gillespie suggests that you write an open letter to stepchildren (Gillespie 2004, 74). A letter sounded like a great idea, so I wrote one similar to the one in the book. The letter went something like this:

> *Dear Brayden,*
>
> *I just wanted to write you a letter to let you know how excited I am to have been chosen to be a part of your life. I know that you didn't ask for a stepmother, and at times it has been hard for you. However, Romans 8:28 is one of my favorite scriptures which says, "All things work together for good for those who love the Lord and are called according to his purpose." This means I believe that God has something special planned for our stepfamily, and he will take the bad things in our life and make them work out okay.*
>
> *You are a smart young man with many talents. I admire the love you have for both your mom and dad. I am not trying to replace either of them, but wanted you to know that if you need me for anything, I am here. Also, if you can think of things that will make our relationship and our family better, I would love to hear your advice. I am hoping that we can begin to do better.*
>
> *Love, Stepmom Janice*

I was excited to mail the letter and hoped and prayed that I would get any type of response from Brayden, which unfortunately never came. When I finally saw Brayden at church, I inquired if he had received the letter. He answered affirmatively, but I saw fear in his eyes of being forced into a conversation. I asked him if he understood what I was trying to say in the letter. He said, "Yes."

I felt like I was pulling teeth so I decided to take him out of his misery and leave well enough alone. I asked him if he had my cell phone number. He said he didn't, so I gave it to him and encouraged him to call whenever he wanted to, but I assured him there was no pressure. I didn't think the letter did much good, so I would try something else later.

A few months later, Bobby and I were out for Valentine's Day when I received a text from Brayden wishing me a Happy Valentine's Day. I was pleasantly surprised and returned the Valentine's Day wishes by text. I sent an additional message inquiring if there was someone special he was planning to spend time with. He responded indicating his interest in a certain young lady. I encouraged him to do something nice for her for Valentine's Day. We went back and forth until I ended the series of texts by indicating how much I enjoyed our text conversation and that we should do it more often. From that point on, I received occasional texts and a few calls asking my advice about girls. Our relationship grew comfortably, and I encouraged him to stay with us whenever he was home from college. He did on several occasions, and we reached an understanding. He knew I was not trying to mother him. Instead I became a support whenever he needed me. I even taught him how to cook broiled Tilapia.

Home Delivery

A postcard came in the mail indicating Brandon would be participating in standardized tests at school. The card suggested parents support their children by making sure they had a hot breakfast, a good night's sleep, and lots of encouragement. I noticed the card as I was leaving the house to go to Wal-Mart to pick up a few items. While at the store, I got the bright idea to put together a care package for Brandon with healthy snacks and a card. I wanted to encourage him and remind him we were thinking of him, and confident in his ability to do well on the tests. It was Sunday evening and he was beginning the testing on Monday morning, so I decided to deliver the package as soon as possible.

I put everything in a gift bag and dropped it off on the bio-mom's porch. On my way home, I placed a call to their home and left a voice mail message indicating the package left on the porch. He called me back before I made it home with a big thank you. I was so excited about what I did I wanted to rush home to tell Bobby. When I walked in the door, the phone was ringing, and the caller ID said it was the kids. I figured that the kids would tell Bobby about my surprise, but no one mentioned it. Later that night I told Bobby what I did. The next day he informed me how thrilled Brandon was about the care package.

The Step Card Collection

I was browsing the Internet one evening and found a website that had on-line cards for stepfamilies (www.thestepcardcollection.com). The website contained personal cards and the like, including birthday cards, and other written expressions for those living-in-step. There was one in particular that caught my eye.

It read: "Sometimes you purposely push my buttons. A) I don't know if it is to get a reaction, B) to test me, or C) because you can't stand me. I hope it's not C. I guess I could push your buttons too and maybe I do, but believe me it's not intentional. The times when we get along are great . . . I wish they were more often."

This card described the relationship between Janae and me so well. I changed the wording a little bit and sent her a similar message by text to her cell phone. The good news is that she assured me it wasn't C. I was grateful and asked if she would meet me for dinner.

Dinner was the perfect opportunity to share what we needed from one another in order to have a better relationship. We offered mutual apologies and agreed to do better. The improvement was immediate, for we began to spend more time together. Janae became an asset to me at church assisting me with youth activities. Previously, we did our best to avoid one another at church, but now we were working together to bless others. Janae is blessed with a number of spiritual gifts, including singing and teaching. God continued to use her to help our youth and music ministries until she was ready to spread her wings and move on to another church.

From then on, Janae and I have continued to build the respectful loving friendship that I have always dreamed of. I value and appreciate her for allowing me to be a part of her life as her stepmom. Our relationship works for us, and I wouldn't trade it for anything. We occasionally get together and have a great time laughing, talking, and discussing any number of subjects. Our favorite topic is her desire to find a Christian man to share her life with.

As I neared the completion of this book, I finally got the courage to ask Janae to read it and offer her opinion. In my asking, I explained my fear of opening old wounds and spoiling the relationship we had worked so hard to build. Guess what? She agreed to read it even though it was painful for her. We discussed the contents of the book over lunch and had an open conversation regarding our experiences as a stepfamily. She asked a lot of questions, shared some valuable insight, and I agreed to make needed changes. Thanks again Janae!

As time went on I tried to be deliberate in my efforts to build relationships with Bobby's children. Some days I was successful, other times, not. At least we had arrived at an understanding that they were not intentionally trying to hurt me. Once I maintained a spirit of forgiveness regarding the past wrongs and extended a measure of grace for future occurrences, our relationships improved. I stopped depending on Bobby to try to fix things between me and his children and assumed the responsibility myself.

With God's help it is possible to forgive. I can't stress enough the power of forgiveness. Being able to forgive Bobby's children did wonders for me. Once I released the pain of the past, I saw our lives differently. I no longer saw myself as the victim of kids who wanted no part of me in their lives. I no longer saw them and the bio-mom as the enemy. Instead God allowed me to see five heartbroken children who were confused and hurting because of parental choices. The emotional and psychological adjustment to their parent's divorce and our re-marriage was underestimated. My goal was to be a positive influence in their lives and make little demands for their loyalty and love. Instead I prayed for compassion and patience to wait until they were ready to allow me a special place in their hearts.

Stepmom Survival Tips

1. Don't blame the individuals in a stepfamily; blame behavior on the cost of living-in-step.
2. Don't dwell on the past and what was done to you. Be willing to strive for forgiveness.
3. Ask God for a spirit of forgiveness and pray continually for God's help.
4. Search the Bible for scriptures on forgiveness and pray and meditate on them.
5. Read a book on forgiveness. Many people have forgiven far worse offenses and freed themselves.
6. Be willing to admit your wrongs and ask for forgiveness.
7. Build a cordial relationship with the bio-mom, offering support and encouragement.
8. Be creative in establishing one-on-one relationships with stepchildren. What works for one may not work for another.
9. Seek professional counseling assistance if needed from a licensed counselor or your pastor, preferably someone who understands the dynamics of stepfamilies.
10. Develop compassion and understanding for the children and the bio-parent. Think about what it would be like to walk in their shoes.

Helpful Scriptures

Hosea 14:4 (NIV)

I will heal their waywardness and love them freely, for my anger has turned away from them.

Psalm 25:11 (NIV)

For the sake of your name, LORD, forgive my iniquity, though it is great.

Genesis 50:17 (NIV)

This is what you are to say to Joseph: I ask you to forgive your brothers the sins and the wrongs they committed in treating you so badly.' Now please forgive the sins of the servants of the God of your father." When their message came to him, Joseph wept.

Jeremiah 33:8 (NIV)

I will cleanse them from all the sin they have committed against me and will forgive all their sins of rebellion against me.

Matthew 6:14-15 (NIV)

For if you forgive other people when they sin against you, your heavenly Father will also forgive you. But if you do not forgive others their sins, your Father will not forgive your sins.

Matthew 18:21-22 (NIV)

Then Peter came to Jesus and asked, "Lord, how many times shall I forgive my brother or sister who sins against me? Up to seven times?" Jesus answered, "I tell you, not seven times, but seventy-seven times.

Chapter Thirteen
Living, Loving, and Learning
One Step at a Time

But those who trust the LORD will find new strength. They will be strong like eagles soaring upward on wings; they will walk and run without getting tired. Isaiah 40:31 (CEV)

Step with Love

In year five of our marriage, we perceived the Lord leading us to share our experiences with others and as a result help other families' living-in-step. Our friends Greg and Beverly White, also stepparents, registered for extensive stepfamily training and invited us to join them. Bobby and I along with the White's, ventured to New York City to be trained in stepfamily dynamics and interventions by stepfamily expert Jeannette Lofas, founder and president of the Stepfamily Foundation, Incorporated. Dr. Lofas' organization was the first in the world devoted solely to the problems and challenges encountered in step relationships. As a stepfamily counselor, Dr. Lofas has personally or by telephone counseled thousands of individuals involved in step relationships and has trained over 10,000 helping professionals. We trained for three days along with other professionals, and as a result, I am a Certified Stepfamily Coach, and

Bobby is a Certified Stepfamily Counselor (Bobby is also a Certified Christian Counselor.)

This training made a world of difference for us and we returned home with a new determination, equipped with practical knowledge and proven techniques specific to the divorced and remarried family system. Later, we also attended a Smart Stepfamily seminar led by stepfamily expert Ron Deal, founder and president of Successful Stepfamilies, a ministry devoted to helping stepfamilies. We immediately put into practice much of what we had learned, and began seeing gradual improvement. Once we understood the differences between stepfamilies and traditional families, our expectations and approach changed significantly, and we saw progress in many of the areas in which we had struggled previously.

Following training, we developed our own stepfamily ministry called Step with Love (www.stepwithlove.org). Our aim is to assist individuals, couples, and families who are preparing for marriage or who are experiencing the challenges of living-in-step. We have taken the principles and methodologies learned from stepfamily experts and combined them with Christian principles to help and serve others. Bobby and I present at premarital conferences and marriage workshops, and Bobby introduced using temperament counseling with stepfamilies to professionals associated with the National Christian Counselors Association. We have been given opportunities to teach stepfamilies the tools to move toward a healthy and successful family. It has been said, "God will take your biggest hurts and turn them in to blessings to be a blessing to others." This is what He has done for us.

Much of what I will share with you in this chapter comes from having a better understanding of what it means to live-in-step. I pray this knowledge will also help you move towards a successful stepfamily.

Stepfamilies Are Different Than Biological Families

The expectation that our new family was to operate like a traditional family was a misconception that contributed to our distress. Whenever you try to operate a stepfamily like a traditional family, you are headed for trouble. Stepfamilies have a much different structure and etiology than biological families. Stepfamilies are born out of loss because parents have experienced the end of a relationship either through divorce, separation, or death. The circumstances surrounding the end of the relationship are rarely joyous. Another very obvious difference is that in a biological family everyone is related by blood. It has never been truer when living-in-step that blood is thicker than water. Medically, when an organ transplant occurs, the recipient's body immediately rejects the new foreign cells. Special medications have to be given to protect the body and the new organ from infection. In a stepfamily, the new marriage mirrors an organ transplant, and the new stepparents are the foreign substance or aliens attempting to invade the established entity. Rejection is natural until the body begins to accept the alien as part of itself. Acceptance of the foreign body takes time. The stepfamily is not afforded time because everyone is thrown into the unit at the same time. In biological families, parenting happens gradually because the couple has time together to build a foundation prior to the birth of children.

In addition, the biological family lives together in one house until children grow up and move on. If everyone lives in one house, there is much less ability to pit parent against parent, and parents back one another up demanding respect for the other parent. Children are bonded to their parents and want to please both of them. Love is natural between parents and children. If there is any competition, it is generally healthy. Parents work for the good of their mutual children. Everyone knows his or her position and role in the family.

In stepfamilies, the parent-child relationship predates the couple's relationship, and there is little time to develop norms. Children are often subjected to fights between parents who live in separate homes and the non-custodial parents and stepparents. Children are often asked to take sides. Stepfamilies come from different backgrounds and, ways of being and seeing the world. These differences again create conflict for the stepfamily. When a traditional family is in trouble, most counselors and even pastors are trained in marriage and family counseling taught in colleges, universities, and seminaries. The immense majority of professionals are not knowledgeable in stepfamily dynamics and management.

Build Couple Strength

Early in our marriage it was Bobby and me against the world. The threat of outside forces caused us to be on the constant lookout for any influence attempting to destroy our marriage. I cannot stress enough that couple's living-in-step, must love and support one another. Remember, the reason you are living in-step in the first place is because you love one another and want to spend the rest of your life together. Let your spouse know you love him and that he is the most important person in your life. Talk to him. Listen to him. Make him feel special.

Make a commitment to stay married. Remember you are one. Do the work to have a flourishing marriage. Take your marriage vows seriously and never allow the word divorce to enter your mind. Celebrate every month/year you are together. Appreciate the value being married brings to your life. Thank God for the spouse he has chosen for you. Speak positively about your spouse to others.

Spend time daily in prayer together. This foundation has kept us strong in the most difficult of times. Every morning before we leave for work, we take the time to pray. We have read couples devotionals together in the morning or at night before going to bed. Establish couple rituals. Bobby and I go walking around the neighborhood regularly, and on Sundays we take a sunset walk around the lake holding hands. We try to keep our dates regardless of what is going on. We enjoy eating popcorn together. We plan to get in the bed at the same time and always kiss goodnight.

Be aware that step-parenting can be hazardous to your sex life. Make time to be alone with your spouse when your stepchildren are present. Establish space boundaries with your children. When your bedroom door is closed, they must understand that you are not to be disturbed. It is okay to show public displays of affection around your children, but don't overdo it. Sometimes, I can still see Bobby's children look the other way when we greet one another with a kiss. Bobby and I were fortunate because we often had every other weekend to ourselves. During our weekends, we ignored the rest of the world and did the things we enjoyed doing together. We go on a honeymoon trip every anniversary and try as much as possible to get away quarterly.

A man's greatest fear can be that he is not being a good father to his children. Keep encouraging him to be a good father and to love his children as only a father can. Don't question when he wants to spend time with his children or wants to spend additional money on them. Don't criticize the way he does things or accuse him of not parenting correctly. Compliment him on his parenting skills and support him in decision making regarding his children. Ask him what you can do to assist him or make his role as a father easier. Recognize and embrace when he needs to be alone with his children without you.

Plan and Organize Your Stepfamily

Unrealistic expectations about your stepfamily can lead to disappointment and resentment. One big happy family is a myth that cannot be achieved. Don't expect instant love. Realize you will love stepchildren differently and don't feel guilty about loving them differently than you love your own children. Your heart is big enough to love everyone uniquely. Be careful to take things slowly and don't try to force relationships. Avoid trying to be Super Stepmom, causing to you feel rejected when you are too overwhelming.

Most stepmoms are career women who have been successful in their careers. We learn how to manage our work life but allow chaos in our stepfamilies. We fail to plan, and therefore, plan to fail. Manage your home with the same close attention you give your career. Write a family mission statement. Set goals for your family. Have a vision of how you would like your family to work and behave. As adults, set the guidelines for your household.

Define what your role will be in your new family. Will you become involved in day to day parenting of your stepchildren? Only two percent of fathers have custody of their children, so most of you will be a non-custodial stepparent. Unfortunately, part-time stepparenting is the most difficult of all scenarios because you have less time to normalize your family and less influence on your stepchildren. How do you want to spend your time when your stepchildren are at your home? Are you comfortable with cooking and cleaning for them? Do you want to be in the middle of their activities, or are you content to let your husband spend much needed time alone with his children? Be careful not to get caught up in the name game of wanting a name without the roles and responsibilities. Decide how you will support your husband during visitation.

Help everyone in your family to understand his or her role in your new family. Remind everyone that he or she is part of a team, and everyone has roles and responsibilities. Encourage mutual respect for one another. Have a family meeting to establish and discuss household rules, such as curfews and assignments of chores. Develop schedules around housekeeping and other chores. Talk about the expectations for everyone in the household. For example, you could say, "In this house, we say please and thank you and clean up after ourselves." Take the emotion out of decision making.

Don't let differences divide you. Remember not to focus on trying to get everyone to do things your way. For instance, I finally figured out there is no right or wrong way to fold towels. You don't have to be right all the time. Don't be anal about things that really don't matter. As Bobby says, "Decide what hill you want to die on and pick your battles wisely." Believe it or not, I finally gave up on the television rules.

Establish new family traditions and rituals. A significant area to establish rituals is to focus on meals. Meals are a frequent activity that allows you to develop structure and establish traditions. Know that holidays can be especially stressful if you do not plan in advance. Avoid confusion by communicating in a positive manner with the bio-parent and sharing your plans. Establish how birthdays will be celebrated. Will you put your differences aside and celebrate the child's birthday with the biological parent, or will you celebrate separately?

For the most part, specifically in the beginning, let your spouse handle the discipline for his children, and you discipline your children. Don't become a tattletale every time his children do something that you do not like or agree with. Help children to understand that actions have consequences and let them participate in deciding what those consequences will be. They are often more severe in their own punishment than you would consider being.

Develop Empathy for Children

Children are often made out to be the bad guys when talking with stepmoms, but actually everyone can become a victim of living-in-step. Children did not ask for their parents to divorce, for a stepparent, or to be shuffled from house to house. We must always realize divorce is devastating, and some children and even adults never recover. Divorce can affect children's self-esteem and may determine their own relationship patterns as they become adults. Remember, stepfamilies are born from loss. Children are not happy to see their parents' divorce and long for them to get back together no matter how miserable they were or how much they argued.

Try to understand divorce and remarriage from a child's perspective, and this knowledge may help you have compassion for them particularly when their behavior is less that what's expected.

Read books written for and about children of divorce. Books have been written for even the youngest of children. Know divorce is not a onetime event for them but an ongoing source of pain and grief. Triggers are everywhere. Each time they come to your house for visitation, old wounds could be re-opened. Remember, children are at least one to two years behind their parent in the grieving process. Children may even experience grief at different stages in their life showing up when you least expect it. Our circumstances were especially complicated, so grieving was prolonged for Bobby's children.

Understand the conflict of loyalties children experience. If they love you as a stepmom, they may believe they are betraying their mother. These conflicts can be emotionally destructive for children. Remind stepchildren you are not trying to take anyone's place. Don't find yourself competing out of insecurity. Don't be indifferent if children share something positive comments about their bio-parent. Celebrate what goes on in the other home. When the bio-mom remarried, we encouraged the children to be happy for her and support the union by participating in the wedding festivities. We did the same when my ex-remarried and supported them by sending a wedding gift.

Encourage Co-Parenting with His Ex

Go beyond what your divorce decree says and make a commitment to work with your ex-spouse or bio-parent to raise resilient children. Even if you are angry at the ex-spouse during and following the divorce, make the decision to forgive and move forward. Don't start arguments with the ex or argue with your spouse's ex. Have a documented co-parenting plan. Make arrangements regarding visitation, birthday parties, graduations, weddings, holidays, and other special occasions, so everyone knows what to expect. Work together instead of against one another engaging in competition.

As mentioned previously, I was successful in communicating with the bio-dad regarding our children. In the years since our divorce, we have had few arguments about our children. Whenever I have something to discuss, I give him advanced warning through a text or email. We schedule time to talk. I do not harbor any resentment as a result of our divorce. We made a mutual decision, and although divorce was painful, I do not blame him for it.

The biological parent has to release his or her children to develop a relationship with a stepparent. Because children have conflicts of loyalty, the biological parent has to encourage and support the relationship. I speak positively of my ex-husband's wife, and complement them as a couple indicating how perfect they are for one another. I also support and encourage a relationship with her daughter. They see all of us interacting positively towards one another. Modeling good behavior is great for the kids.

Bobby wasn't quite so fortunate when it came to working with the bio-mom, yet I encouraged him to work with her as best he could. We even prayed for her on several occasions as decisions were being made and when we knew there were areas of potential conflict. If there is conflict with the ex, don't badmouth them. Badmouthing the other parent is not good for the children, for it causes confusion and can lead to low self-esteem. Never put the child in the middle. Teach children to honor each parent's point of view. Don't try to influence them to take your side. If the child bad-mouths the other parent, remind him or her to respect and honor his or her parent. If you don't have anything good to say about the other parent, keep your mouth shut.

When Conflict Comes

Wherever there are differences, there will be conflict. When it comes, and it will come, handle it without causing permanent damage to your relationship with your spouse and your stepchildren. Learn to accept the things you cannot change and use discernment when deciding what things to confront. Remember, you can't fix what you think is wrong with children in a weekend, and it is not your responsibility to change them.

The number one conflict in stepfamilies is related to the children, and the second is money. Ask for God's guidance on how to communicate regarding difficult issues. Discuss finances openly and decide how money is to be spent. Make agreements in advance. Realize that following divorce, one's finances are most likely unstable and damaged. Don't judge.

Don't allow Satan to use you to destroy your family. Avoid taking everything personally. Blame living-in-step, not the persons involved. Learn to fight fair. Listen to your spouse. Discuss what you see and not what you feel. Don't bring up the past or keep a ledger of wrongs. Be a Godly woman and ask God for his help when you want to lash out at others. Set the example for children on how to resolve differences.

Even when you are badmouthed or attacked, do as Laura Petherbridge suggests and "Let the bullet bounce." That means put on your shield or thick skin when cruel, unfair, and hurtful comments are fired at you. Pray for those who speak and intend evil against you. It won't feel good sometimes and you will feel abused, but allow God to fight your battles. "Vengeance is mine," saith the Lord.

Forgive, Forgive, and Forgive Again

I wish I could say that your stepchildren or even your spouse will never do or say anything that deeply offends you, but they will, time and time again. It may be as simple as not including you or sometimes downright ignoring you. However, no matter what happens, let love be your guide. Have compassion and always be ready to forgive, even when you have been wronged. I Corinthians 13:4-6 encourages us to remember that love is patient and kind and does not keep a record of wrongdoings. Read a book on forgiveness and pray for guidance on how to release you from the bondage of anger and unforgiveness. In my reading, I ran across a wonderful book that examines the relationship between unforgiveness and illness. In the conclusion of his book *The Forgiveness Project*, Dr. Michael Barry makes the following statement about forgiveness: "The goal of forgiveness, therefore, is to replace toxic feelings of hatred with the more life-giving, nonlethal, neutral feeling of love. This feeling is being born out of a well-meaning, peaceful indifference that allows us to wish the best-and mean it-for those who have harmed us" (Barry 2011, 104). His book was such a blessing to me that I placed a personal call to him to see if I could learn the techniques of his forgiveness training called Release. He not only shared with me, he also agreed to come to our church and present a forgiveness seminar. What a blessing.

Get and Provide Support

When I have an opportunity to listen to another stepmom, one of two things happens. I either receive hope and encouragement by learning from her experiences, or I realize that my situation isn't so bad after all and could be a whole lot worse. It was a relief to hear others were experiencing some of the same issues, emotions, and challenges we experienced. If you have not married yet, read and learn as much as you can about stepfamilies so that you can avoid making some of the mistakes that we made. Get premarital counseling that addresses the unique dynamics of stepfamilies before you begin your marriage. Look on the internet and read blogs written by other stepmoms. Avoid those that take every opportunity to complain and speak negatively about husbands, stepchildren, or even the bio-mom.

If you are a new stepmom and did not have a clue about the complexities of living-in-step, seek out others who have been married for a while and have developed and built couple strength, living successfully in step. If you are already a pro at being a stepmom, take the time to encourage and bless another stepmom. Share tools and experiences that are encouraging and helpful. Send a card or a letter, cheering a new stepmom on. Buy her a copy of this book.

One of our ambitions is to help churches develop step ministries to assist in building healthy families. Couples who are involved in couples' ministries sponsored through churches have less risk of divorcing. Divorce rates for Christians and non-Christians are similar; however, there are very few churches that offer specialized services for stepfamilies. Consider starting a stepmom support group at your church. I applaud Ron Deal for conducting Smart Family workshops at churches.

If you are experiencing problems in your marriage, seek the help of a counselor or coach who specializes in stepfamilies. The Stepfamily Foundation's website (www.Stepfamily.org) offers a list of stepfamily services and experts nationwide. You can probably find one in your area or one who offers telephone coaching as I do. Encourage your pastor to receive specialized training in stepfamily dynamics. Finally, read books written by other stepmoms who have traveled down this lonely road. Receive encouragement from reading and hearing their stories. Most stepmoms complain of having no resources. Get out there and find the help you need. Lastly, you are not alone. With 1,300 new families forming every day, stepfamilies are becoming the new normal. Don't give up on your marriage. Continue to live, love and learn, one step at a time.

Helpful Scriptures

Proverbs 18:16 (NIV)
A gift opens the way and ushers the giver into the presence of the great.

Philippians 4:11 (CEV)
I am not complaining about having too little. I have learned to be satisfied with whatever I have.

Matthew 6:6 (MSG)
Here's what I want you to do: Find a quiet, secluded place so you won't be tempted to role-play before God. Just be there as simply and honestly as you can manage. The focus will shift from you to God, and you will begin to sense his grace.

Ephesians 2:7-10 (MSG)
Now God has us where he wants us, with all the time in this world and the next to shower grace and kindness upon us in Christ Jesus. Saving is all his idea, and all his work. All we do is trust him enough to let him do it. It's God's gift from start to finish! We don't play the major role. If we did, we'd probably go around bragging that we'd done the whole thing! No, we neither make nor save ourselves. God does both the making and saving. He creates each of us by Christ Jesus to join him in the work he does, the good work he has gotten ready for us to do, work we had better be doing.

1 Samuel 10:7 (CEV)
After these things happen, do whatever you think is right! God will help you.

Psalm 81:10 (CEV)
I am the LORD your God. I rescued you from Egypt. Just ask, and I will give you whatever you need.

Notes from the Author

Finally, brethren, whatsoever things are true, whatsoever things are honest, whatsoever things are just, whatsoever things are pure, whatsoever things are lovely, whatsoever things are of good report; if there be any virtue, and if there be any praise, think on these things. Philippians 4:8 (KJV)

A Decade of Love

With half of new marriages failing and two thirds of re-marriages ending in divorce, particularly if they involve children from a previous relationship, Bobby and I are thankful to God that we have now been married over ten years. As I began to write the conclusion of this book, a life changing event happened in the life of our stepfamily members. Not long before Thanksgiving 2010, the bio-mom was diagnosed with cancer. After aggressive treatment and fighting it for the sake of her children, she succumbed to lung cancer in October of 2011. Things have changed significantly for us, but God is able. Brayden, Jamie, and Brandon now live with us, and our roles are much different as custodial parents. I entered this new chapter with a fear of the unknown, but God has given me peace that he will not leave me or forsake me. Please pray for our family as we are still in transition.

Although we are in unchartered territory helping Bobby's children through their grief, we know that all things work together for good. We are waiting on God's promises to be fulfilled in our lives. We are optimistic for what the future holds for our family. Our children are growing up faster than we ever imagined, and seven out of eight are adults now. In just a few years we will be empty nesters and preparing to be step grandparents.

I am thankful for my husband for loving me, for accepting me, and for allowing me to stepparent his six wonderful children the best I knew how. He has been much more patient with me than I ever could imagine. I will forever be grateful for his love and support. My prayer is I have helped him to be an even better parent and role model for his children. Our joint prayer has been that our children will learn from our mistakes and view our union as encouragement to find the person God has chosen for them.

Called to be a Stepmom

Being a stepmom to six children was an overwhelming challenge for me, but once I realized I didn't just stumble into this role, and God had plans for my family, I quit trying to control myself, my husband, and our children. I finally had to surrender and accept the lessons God had for me. I am thankful for God's grace and mercy; otherwise, I would not have been able to share my experiences with anyone. Throughout this journey, I have learned God will never put more on us than we can bear and will give us peace that surpasses all understanding.

The good news about being a stepmom is the longer you are married, the better your marriage and stepfamily become. Most stepfamily books suggest it takes seven years to see a significant improvement. This prediction was true for us, but the change came mainly because we turned the situation over to God and asked for his help. For those of you considering this journey, make sure you have spent much time in prayer and lengthy discussions with your future mate before becoming a stepmom. It would also be helpful to attend pre-marital counseling sessions with someone trained in stepfamily dynamics. Step mothering is not for the faint or for one who thinks she can do this alone. Don't assume because you are a great mom you will have guaranteed success as a stepmom. Make sure you take God with you into the marriage and consult him daily for direction.

Some of you are already in the trenches and seeking someone to understand what you are going through. I hope this book has been helpful, and you will use it as a resource for living-in-step. Share this book with your spouse and other stepmoms. We also encourage you to visit our website at www.Stepwithlove.org for additional tools to help your stepfamily. You may send confidential e-mails to jlove@stepwithlove.org.

Resources & References

Barry, Michael. *The Forgiveness Project: The Startling Discovery of How to Overcome Cancer, Find Health, and Achieve Peace.* Grand Rapids, Michigan: Kregal Publications, 2011.

Clark, Terri. *Tying the Family Knot: Meeting the Challenges of a Blended Family.* Nashville, Tennessee: Broadman & Holman Publishers, 2004.

Clurman, Ruth-Ann. *Parenting the Other Chick's Eggs: A Helpful and Entertaining Guide for How to Build a Strong and Loving Blended Family.* Shawnee Mission, Kansas: National Press Publications, 1997.

Colino, Stacey. "The Stress of Ambivalent Feelings." *Shape Magazine,* May 1, 2005.

Deal, Ron and Laura Petherbridge. *The Smart Stepmom.* Grand Rapids, Michigan: Bethany House Publishers, Baker Publishing Group, 2009.

Deal, Ron L. *The Smart Step-Family: Seven Steps to a Healthy Family.* Minneapolis, Minnesota: Bethany House, 2002.

Gillespie, Natalie Nichols. *The Stepfamily Survival Guide.* Grand Rapids, Michigan: Baker Publishing Group, 2004.

Hallowell, Edward M. *Dare to Forgive, The Power of Letting Go & Moving On.* Deerfield Beach, Florida: Health Communications, Inc., 2004

Holt-Lunstad, Julianne, Bert N Uchino, Timothy W Olson, Chrisana Olson-Cerny, and Jill B Nealey-Moore. *"Social relationships and ambulatory blood pressure: Structural and qualitative predictors of cardiovascular functioning during every day social interactions. ioe."* Health Psychology, 2003: 388-397.

Houpe, Steve and Donna Houpe. *Becoming One Family: Bringing Blended Families Together.* Tulsa, Oklahoma: Harrison House, 2009.

Kass, Anne. *Second Marriage Can Be as Difficult as the First.* Nolo.com., www.alllaw.com/articles/family/divorce/article49.asp (accessed June 25, 2010.

Kids First Center, *What Kids Want Grown Ups to Know about Separation and Divorce.* Standish, Maine: Tower Publishing, 2008.

Leman, Kevin. *Living in a Stepfamily Without Getting Stepped On.* Nashville, Tennessee: Thomas Nelson Publishers, 1994.

Lofas, Jeannette. *Everything You Need to Know to Make It Work,* (Revised and Updated). New York, New York: Citadel Press Books, Kensington Publishing Corporation, 2004.

Lofas, Jeannette. Family Rules: *Helping Stepfamilies and Single Parents Build Happy Homes.* New York, New York: Kensington Publishing Corp., 1998.

Lutz, Ericka. *The Complete Idiot's Guide to Stepparenting.* New York, New York: Penguin Group, 1998.

Parrott, Les and Leslie Parrott. *Saving Your Second Marriage Before it Starts.* Grand Rapids, Michigan: Zondervan, 2001.

Richardson, Cheryl. *The Unmistakable Touch of Grace*. New York, New York: Simon & Schuster, 2005.

Roosevelt, Ruth and Jeannette Lofas. *Living in Step: A Remarriage Manual For Parents and Children*. New York, NY: The Stepfamily Foundation, 1976.

Stewart, Susan D. *Brave New Stepfamilies: Diverse Paths Toward Stepfamily Living*. Thousand Oaks, California: Sage Publications, Inc., 2007.

Visher, Emily B. and John S. Visher. *Therapy With Stepfamilies*. New York: Brunner/Mazel, Inc., 1996.

Wallerstein, Judith D., Julia M. Lewis, Sandra Blakeslee. *The Unexpected Legacy of Divorce: A 25 year Landmark Study*. New York, New York: Hyperion, 2000.

Notes

Please feel free to write down your thoughts, feelings, hopes, plans, and key ideas from the book in this area

⊰⊱

Notes

Notes

Notes

Notes

Notes

Notes

Notes

Notes

Notes

Notes

Notes

Notes

Janice R. Love

Notes

About the Author

Photo ©Portraits Today Studios

Janice R. Love, is the biological mother of two children and has been the stepmother of six children for over ten years. Janice earned a Master's in Psychology from the University of Oklahoma and has been trained and certified as a Stepfamily Certified Coach by the Stepfamily Foundation Incorporated in New York City. Mrs. Love and her husband Rev. Dr. Bobby L. Love, are the founders of Step With Love, a ministry that offers Blended Family Counseling, Coaching and seminars for couples, stepmoms and churches respectively. They live in Olathe, Kansas, along with three of his children. For more information about this book, visit www.janicelovebooks.com, or about their stepfamily ministry, visit www.stepwithlove.org.

www.ingramcontent.com/pod-product-compliance
Lightning Source LLC
LaVergne TN
LVHW051549080426
835510LV00020B/2920